DYING TO EAT

CONFESSIONS OF A FOOD ADDICT

ED ADAMS
ZANDY DUDIAK

Published by LoneDog Press
Turtle Creek, PA 15145

Printed in the USA

2019 Editions - Print & eBook

Cover Art: Jonathan Holiday

Dedication and Acknowledgments

Dying to Eat: Confessions of a Food Addict is dedicated to our family members and friends who have been there for us through our ups and downs, and especially Ed's mom, Nelda Adams, for her unwavering love.

With special thanks to Rev. Doug Rehberg, Susan Seibel, Carol Polidora, Renea Mason, Lillian DeDomenic, Kyle Jenkins, and Pete Farkasovsky.

"Built along the lines of a smaller Bob Robertson, Penn Hills first baseman Ed Adams no doubt will be a hot Major League prospect one of these days."
    — *Bob Black, The Pittsburgh Press, June 1977*

"Ed was a natural hitter. He was the best. He could have gone a long way."
    — *Len Gallo, Little League coach*

"He was a great hitter, I mean a really great hitter. He actually had a Major League swing."
    — *Frank Mazzei, American Legion coach*

"Ed could have been a designated hitter for the American Baseball League."
    — *Bob Ford, coach and teacher, Penn Hills High School*

"I figured he'd be our next star going to the big leagues. He was a good fielder and a tremendous hitter. Yet he was humble, mannerly, and nice to talk to."
    — *Ralph Valerio, sports editor, Gateway Newspapers*

"Eddie didn't hit the ball, he mashed it, his powerful lower body giving him the ability to launch balls high into the Western Pennsylvania night. Although we fell one game shy of the state championship in 1977, it was Eddie's leadership that helped pave the way for our 1978 state title team. He showed us all how to win, and maybe more importantly, how to play the game with passion and dignity."
    — *Dave Droschak, Penn Hills High School Class of 1978, Springfield (Ill.) Cardinals, Associated Press sports editor*

1

UP TO BAT

More than 6,000 excited fans watched me from the home field bleachers as I walked up to the plate. I was the designated hitter for the University of South Carolina Gamecocks that hot and humid Sunday in April 1978.

People were everywhere—the most I'd ever seen at a non-Major League baseball game. The size of the crowd at "The Roost," as the field was called, wasn't surprising, though. The rivalry between the Gamecocks and the Clemson University Tigers is one of the biggest in the nation.

In the bottom of the eighth inning, we were up by three runs. Because of the heat and humidity, we were told in the dugout to take our time, to stall as much as possible to give our relief pitcher, Hal Gaalema, a chance to rest and cool off so he could finish strong in the ninth inning.

While on deck, I took a look through the bleachers. I had been in crowds like these as a kid, watching all sorts of sporting events. Now, all eyes were on me after the leadoff hitter made an out. The crowd blurred from my sight as excitement and nervousness raced through my body. All I could think about was this pitcher, who threw pretty hard.

I walked toward the plate, remembering what the coach said in the dugout. As I approached the batter's box, I asked the umpire for time-out. I walked back to the on-deck circle and put more pine tar on the wooden bat, then untied and retied my left spike to buy more time.

Enough stalling. I headed back to the plate—to one of my favorite things in the world. When it came to hitting a baseball, I knew just what to do. Keep my eyes on the ball, my back foot planted, stride right at the pitcher, and swing level.

Just like my dad taught me.

There was nothing else for which I was more prepared and no place on earth I would rather be. I watched two pitches go by. My heart beat like a piston. I swung at the third pitch.

Cr-rack. I knew I had hit it well.

I ran toward first base and watched as the ball cleared the right field fence—a home run. Suddenly, I was the reason 6,000 Gamecock fans were screaming. A tingle ran through my body. As I cleared first and trotted to second, the whole scene became surreal for me—like I was watching myself round the bases.

———

I was winded. My heart beat fast.

I hated being the center of attention. By walking quickly, fewer people would see me and snicker as I went to the men's room. The Friday night crowds at the Pizza Hut in Monroeville, Pa. were always huge. After finishing in the bathroom, I walked quickly past the seating line and the entrance to the dining room. All eyes were on me, or so it seemed. I rounded the corner quickly and returned to my safe, incon-spicuous place in the kitchen.

I munched on a piece of pepperoni Pan Pizza as I stuffed another load of dinner plates into the dishwasher. Then I had a brilliant idea. If I pretended to take an order for a large Pan Pizza, it would sit there and no one would pick it up. They let employees take those home for free.

What a genius I was! As I took another bite of pizza, I imagined what toppings I would heap on the phantom order. As I removed the clean, wet dishes from the machine, I couldn't think of anything in the world I'd rather do than eat a pizza after work.

———

W ithin two short years of the excitement of playing NCAA Division I baseball, the absolute peak of my athletic career, I was a 300-pound dishwasher. I wish I could say that this was my bottom—that I lost weight, got married, and had a normal happily-ever-after life. But over the next two decades, things got only worse. My weight more than doubled, and the resulting loneliness and embarrassment created a void that only food could fill. I've been given tools to help me overcome all that holds me back.

But each time, I find myself at war once again with the addict inside.

Being addicted to eating means leading a double life. The phony one is driven by the addiction; the genuine one is buried by it. Recovery is about uncovering your true self—the one God intends the world to see.

My story is exactly that struggle.

Each day, I strive to be more of the person I really am, more a child of God and less someone who has a deviant relationship with food.

2

LITTLE ACE

Food, sports, and my dad. Looking back, perhaps no three things have had a more profound impact on my life. They have been my centers, my anchors, my strengths. When one was missing, another filled the void for me, sometimes in a healthy way, other times not.

Even in one of my earliest memories, a father-son picnic held to celebrate my graduation from kindergarten, all three contributed to making it a perfect day.

I vividly remember munching on a chipped ham sandwich with ketchup, made with Town Talk bread, as I sat with my dad on the lawn of Penn Hills Presbyterian Church. No moms were invited that day, just dads and their sons. I loved being the center of my dad's attention.

I was sporting a black eye, though now I don't remember how it happened. The bruise didn't escape the attention of Mrs. Alice Walker, though. She was a kind teacher who lived in our neighborhood and was in charge of the day's festivities. At one point, she began announcing each graduate's name and told everyone a little about them. When Mrs. Walker came to me, "Eddie Adams," she was quick to point out my shiner to the audience. More importantly, she branded me "the best pitcher in Hamil Hunter Park," the plan of homes where I lived.

It was the first time I had been recognized in public for my athletic talent. And I liked it.

I was born on June 24, 1959 to Edward "Ace" and Nelda Adams. My dad, an athletic man who fit the description of "tall, dark and handsome" to a T, was a police officer for the City of Pittsburgh. My mom, a slender, pretty woman, was a homemaker. They took me home from Magee Women's Hospital in Pittsburgh to Broadhead Street, where rows of narrow houses stood closely side-by-side, touching the sidewalks in front and with small yards in back. Both my parents had grown up in this neighborhood known as Lincoln-Lemington, and it is where they chose to settle after they married on October 25, 1952. In those older city neighborhoods, families were close. My older brother, Lee, and I had doting grandparents nearby—my mom's parents just next door, and my dad's mom just a few blocks away.

Interestingly, it was me, not their first born, Lee, who was christened with my father's name. Lee was named to honor my father's brother, who was killed while serving overseas during World War II. He had the fair complexion and reddish-blond hair that ran on my mother's side of the family. I, on the other hand, was my father's son from top to bottom. Except that I had ice-blue eyes and his were hazel, there was no question I belonged to Ace Adams.

Although policemen were required to live within the city limits, my dad was a World War II vet who wanted a better life for his growing family. He took a risk by deciding to move us to the suburbs. To maintain the residency requirement, he used the Verona Boulevard address where his mother lived. From that point on, Dad would frequently request to be transferred from station to station to avoid anyone catching on to the fact that he lived elsewhere. With the help of his friends, Dad built us a new house in Penn Hills, a large-but-friendly community bordering on the east end of Pittsburgh. We moved there when I was just one year old. The red brick house on quiet Jay Drive quickly became home.

Hamil Hunter Park looked like a typical suburban plan to most people, but for me, the neighborhood was more than houses. It was a stadium. Streets, backyards, and open lots transformed into the field of the day, depending on the sport of the season. Bases, end zones, yard markers, and foul lines were painted, or drawn with chalk or rocks. When the Wiffle ball had cracked beyond its use, I made a new ball from scratch using paper and tape. My friends and I upset many a neighbor with balls flying off their houses and into their yards. When the football game on TV was played in the rain, we hosed down the backyard and played our own game. When the Olympics were on television, we held our own, complete with multiple events and mock TV interviews.

Baseball, basketball, football—it didn't matter. I liked them all. If Mario Lemieux had hit the ice with the Pittsburgh Penguins fifteen years earlier than he did, I most likely would have taken up hockey, too. The neighborhood gang had a big influence on my love of sports. But not as much as my dad.

As a young child, I often went to the ballfields to see my dad play. But given my age, I was more interested in the snow cone cart than what was happening in the game. Many people have told me that Dad was a great ballplayer. He played in the Pittsburgh Fraternal Order of Police League and was selected as an all-star every year. The all-star team played at the famed Forbes Field in Oakland, then home of the Pittsburgh Pirates. I've learned by talking to his friends that he even tried out for the Major Leagues, though he never shared that with me.

It's not a surprise that he had me swinging a bat from the time I could hold one. Our home movies show him patiently, lovingly pitching ball after ball to Lee when he was a toddler. I'm sure he did the same with David and me. Dad taught us everything about sports.

Not only did Dad encourage our own sports abilities, he also gave us the chance to see other athletes in action. It was rare for us to miss the Tuesday and Friday night Penn Hills High School varsity basketball games. The Penn Hills Indians had spawned a number of NCAA Division I players, including George Karl, who went on to play for the University of North Carolina Tar Heels and professionally for the San Antonio Spurs before starting a renowned career as an NBA coach. When Dad's job required him to work security at a sports event in Pittsburgh, he made sure his boys could go, too. We often saw the

Pittsburgh Pirates play at Forbes Field and watched pro-wrestling matches at the Civic Arena.

I emulated my sports heroes—the windmill-batting style of the Pittsburgh Pirates' Willie Stargell and the sharpshooting skills of the L.A. Lakers' Jerry West. I even had New York Jets quarterback Joe "Willie" Namath's #12 on my sixth-grade football jersey and wore white tennis shoes, which were his trademark and quite unusual for the time. But there was another sports hero whom I admired every bit as much—Ace Adams. By the time I was old enough to join Little League and school teams, my dad's friends were already calling me "Little Ace." I looked like him, talked like him, aspired to play like him. I was proud to share his name.

The greatest thing about my early sports career was that Dad was there. He coached our Little League teams, came to my basketball and football games, and served as my personal coach. On the way home after a game, he always pointed out what I did well and what needed work. He switched Lee and me to be left-handed batters. According to him, lefties had an advantage. Time proved him right.

As Lee and I played more, sports became the center of our family life. Mom came to the games a lot, bundling up my sister Jody and brother David, who were two and six years younger than me, respectively, so they could sit through the chilly spring baseball and nippy fall football games. Often, my grandparents came along, too.

As a policeman, Dad worked different shifts. When he was home, the neighborhood kids loved to pile into our light green Pontiac convertible, top down, and head toward the nearest ballfield. In the winter, Dad took the whole Little League team to my elementary school to practice baseball and basketball. The only bad thing about those practice sessions was knowing we'd have to quit and go home. The practice paid off. Our team, the Astros, went two seasons without losing a game—forty-six straight games to be exact.

Having a winning Little League team wasn't enough for my dad. He made playing for him like celebrating a holiday, creating an enthusiastic spirit that helped as much as our talents to make us winners. Because the Astros had white-and-orange uniforms, Dad painted part

With his dad as coach, Ed learned the game of baseball as a member of the Astros.

of all the bats orange. He had the team moms sew orange things on their clothing and make orange pennants. We even had orange water in the water cooler. Going that extra step to make the game special is something my brothers and I continued to do for our teams through the years.

In our society, the cultural norm is to intertwine the joy of celebration with the joy of eating. My dad definitely subscribed to that norm. Sometimes, the team celebrated victories at McDonald's or Dairy Queen. At the end of the year, the crowning moment was the Penn Hills Baseball banquet at the nationally-known Holiday House supper club in nearby Monroeville. Along with winning the championship trophy, we got a great meal, too. Food wasn't a problem for me then. In fact, quite the opposite. As hard as it is to believe, as a kid I was ribs-sticking-out skinny.

"You better eat some more potatoes, boy," I remember my dad telling me one day at the field. And I did.

I had other favorite foods and number one on the list was pizza. The best pizza in town was Della Sala's. It was always a part of the gathering when Len Gallo, who coached the team with my dad, and his family visited or entertained us at their home. Sometimes, we competed to see how many pieces we could eat. I remember having twelve one evening. The pizza shop had a sign announcing that the record was thirty slices in one sitting. I remember thinking that maybe I could break that record someday.

I loved competition and still do. That competitive soul of an athlete has remained the very essence of my being, whether on the ballfield, academically, or struggling to lose hundreds of pounds over and over again.

3

SLIDING INTO HOME

J ust as winter turned to spring and the 1971 Little League baseball season was about to get underway, life threw me and my family a curve ball.

On his way home from work on a Friday in late March, Dad stopped at the local supermarket to pick up an order of groceries for the weekend. While there, he started getting bad chest pains and drove himself to the office of our family physician. The doctor advised Dad to get to a nearby hospital as soon as possible. To the best of our knowledge, he drove himself there as well. Sometime after he arrived, Dad suffered a massive heart attack. The medical team worked frantically for about an hour and a half to bring him back—and finally succeeded. But it was only a short reprieve from death.

Mom was shocked when the hospital doctor told her that Dad, who was only 42, had a rotten heart—like that of a seventy- or eighty-year-old—and that they didn't expect him to live. She came from a strong Roman Catholic background and believed in the Almighty.

"You're not God," she snapped, with firm conviction, at the doctor.

Surrounded by other medical colleagues in the room, the doctor did not respond.

At five-foot-ten, Dad weighed about 220 pounds and carried some mid-section bulk. The fact he was a two-pack-a-day smoker didn't help either. But, none of that mattered now. Ace Adams' days were numbered.

Mom visited him in the hospital every evening for twenty-eight days. The one exception was a day when he was working out the family's financial future with a police department representative. When my mom arrived to visit him, my dad yelled at her to go home. In those days, finances were a man's responsibility, and although Mom would eventually have the burden of providing for four children, for some reason he didn't want her there for the arrangements.

We kids never had a clue that Dad wouldn't be coming home again. In fact, I wasn't exactly sure what was wrong with him. I just knew that baseball season was only a few weeks away and we weren't getting to the field to practice.

The family went to see him on Good Friday. I saw him for the last time when Len Gallo snuck Lee and me through a side door for another visit. I was only eleven, so at the time, the visit didn't strike me as odd. I think he just wanted to see his older boys one more time. He had spent a lot of time with Lee and me, coaching us, teaching us. We were both on the verge of having the fruits of all those years of baseball practice finally pay off. He must have hurt terribly to think he might not be there to share it with us.

Dad died on Wednesday, April 14, 1971, just about two months before my twelfth birthday. I got up for school that cool spring morning, wiped my eyes open, and walked to the edge of the living room, where I saw my mom sitting with two of my dad's friends. I thought it strange that Jim Stitt and Al Cafazzo were at the house so early in the morning.

"Mom, I need some pants," I blurted out.

Startled, my mom led me back to my bedroom and sat me on the bed. Her face had a worried expression and her words were simple and to the point.

"Eddie, Daddy's gone to Heaven."

I was stunned. I knew what that meant. I just lay on the bed, burst into tears and sobbed—deep, heart-wrenching sobs that racked my skinny body. My life changed dramatically in an instant. My hero, my dad, would never throw another ball to me, never guide me, never wipe away my tears, never prepare me for manhood, never see me fulfill his dreams for me.

Although my family was still there for me, a part of me has been alone ever since that day. His death left a void that I have spent decades trying to fill.

Visitation was held at a funeral home owned by friends of my parents in the old Lincoln-Lemington neighborhood. Lee, Jody, David, and I kept going up to the kneeler and just staring. Seeing Dad's lifeless body in the casket disturbed me. I kept wanting his chest to go up and down, and for him to wake up. The adults tried their best to protect the four of us from the reality before us. To take our minds off things, Lee, some friends, and I were sent upstairs to watch basketball games on the color TV.

Most of the Little League team members showed up to pay their last respects to the man who had been like a second father to them. And, just as we always did for someone who had a great game, the guys all signed a baseball and put it, along with a bat and glove, beside Dad in the casket.

The funeral took place on an overcast Saturday at a Lutheran church, which was next door to the funeral home. My dad was not a churchgoing man, but this was his family church. The church pastor delivered the eulogy—and I remember thinking that he didn't know my dad at all. I wished that someone who was close to my Dad had been the one to pay tribute to him.

Six of Dad's friends were pallbearers. As we left the church, it almost looked like a parade as police cars and policemen lined both sides of the street, paying respect to their fallen brother. On the short drive to the cemetery in Penn Hills, it finally dawned on me that this was it—Dad really was never coming home again. His sister, my Aunt Margie, sat next to me in the car and held me while I cried.

The cars rounded the hilly, sharp turns as they approached the cemetery plot where he would be buried next to my grandfather, also Edward M. Adams, who died in 1954. As if Heaven were crying with us, rain started to fall on the large crowd gathered under umbrellas for the graveside service. Fittingly, just a few hundred yards away from Dad's hillside resting place was the field where we'd won the Little League championship just two short years before. As the service concluded and we started back to the cars, Mr. Gallo took my shoulders in his hands and looked me straight in the eyes.

"You are the men of the family now," he told me and Lee. "You have to take care of your mom."

Back at our house for the wake, I grew upset. It bothered me that people acted like it was a party, that they were eating, drinking, and even laughing. Didn't they know my dad was dead? I had to get out of there.

I recruited my cousin Mike from Cincinnati, who was my age. We changed into playclothes and walked to play basketball at the home of neighbors attending the wake. The Wagners wouldn't mind if we used their hoop. I just didn't want to use the one Dad had installed in our backyard . . . not with all those people there. For what seemed like the longest time, Mike and I played one-on-one in the rain without saying a word. Releasing my frustrations through a game I loved seemed to be the only way I could cope with my grief that day.

My memories of the next few weeks are hazy. Friends and neighbors went out of their way to be nice to us, sending cards and bringing food so Mom wouldn't have to cook. Mom kept us out of school for a week. To pass the time, we alternated between our house and the Arndts, two doors down.

To be honest, my family shut down emotionally after dad's death. He was the breadwinner, the disciplinarian, the rock. Mom was simply mortified at the hand life dealt her, but she did everything she could to keep the family going, even learning to drive when she didn't want to. But when it came to grieving, we all went to our own corners. It was more than twenty years later, when I was undergoing in-patient treatment for my eating addiction, that we, for the first time, sat as a family and discussed Dad's death.

Somehow, I had to move forward. The Little League season was almost at hand and Dad's death left us without a manager. Mr. Stitt, who was always very considerate, agreed to move up to fill Dad's shoes, even though his own son, Keith, had advanced to Pony League, the next level of play. I found it difficult to manage the conflicting emotions of losing Dad and being excited about the season getting underway.

We'd won 46 straight games during the previous two years. This was my last year in Little League, and I was ready to do my part to make sure we had another undefeated year. For the first three games of the season, the Astros kept the momentum going. Then came the jinx. Positive that we couldn't lose, someone had decided to get a cake with a big "50" on it to celebrate our 50th consecutive undefeated game. You guessed it. We lost—and ate the cake anyway. We lost a couple of other games, too, but still won the Little League championship for the third straight year with a 20-4 record. Somehow, I think Dad was watching from above and smiling.

I latched onto sports after Dad's death because it was what I knew, what I loved, and it provided a connection to him. I quit football, devoting all my energies to baseball and basketball. The neighborhood stadium had games going almost daily and I practiced a lot on my own. One at a time, I'd hit bucketfuls of rocks into the woods with a bat. I'd shoot 500 foul shots in the snow. I played on every baseball and basketball team that I could. I wanted to be the best because it would have pleased my dad. It also helped me not miss him so much.

I practiced for endless hours and did what he taught me. The athletic success I had was very important to me. It was the largest part of my identity and I think Dad would have been proud. I always felt cheated, though. He wasn't there to see me, as he had always been. Although sports helped teach me about life and being a man, part of me was lost.

Not long after Dad's death, I saw the movie *Born Free* on television for the first time. To this day it brings a tear to my eye. The scene in which Elsa, the lion cub, is set free in the wilderness, and chases after the Jeep, wondering why they are leaving her, just blows me away. Left to fend for herself, Elsa was largely defenseless. I could relate to her so well. It so reminds me of being abandoned by my father.

Though I still had Mom, as one of the older children, I was pretty much like Elsa—on her own in the world. When George and Joy Adamson, the husband-and-wife team who worked as game wardens in East Africa, went back to get Elsa, she was battered, lost, injured—a real mess.

Even though my scars were not visible ones, I was a real mess, too.

4

THE WONDER YEARS

My childhood ended the day Dad died. I stood on the brink of puberty without him there to guide and influence my life. Mom tried hard to fill his shoes, but it was an impossible task.

My twelfth birthday marked a huge turning point in my life. I was going to a different school, I had to change baseball teams, and it was a lot of change to deal with. The timing for all the changes was particularly bad if you factor in adolescence and take away my father's guiding influence. I learned when I got older that change can be good, but at this point in my life it was too much—I didn't have the tools I needed to cope.

I needed an anchor. I found it in sports. It kept a very real connection to my father, and it helped bridge the gap with all the change in front of me.

I decided to drop football, even though I played well, and focus my energies on basketball and baseball. Lord knows, two of my favorite things in life were hitting a baseball and shooting hoops. Seneca Junior High didn't have a baseball team, so I concentrated on hoops while I was there.

On a cold winter afternoon in January 1973, I was a starter for the

Seneca Braves against our cross-town rival, the Penn Junior Eagles. Dick Misenhelter, the high school coach, was in the stands. The game was even in the first half and I made a half-court shot at the buzzer. Penn Junior pulled ahead in the second half and won the game. I wasn't happy that we lost, but I was thrilled that Coach Mise had seen me play a good game.

Baseball, though, was still my first love. I wanted to be on Len Gallo's team the summer after seventh grade, when I joined Pony League. His team of 13- and 14-year-olds was good and had last pick in the drafts. I purposely messed up during tryouts so no other team would want me. But my plan didn't work. I was already too well known. I was picked first in the draft by a team called the Badgers. I didn't know anyone, including the coach.

He was nice but knew little about the game and even less about teaching it to youngsters. When he tried to tell me how to bat, I told him, "I was taught a different way." No way he was gonna mess with the swing that Dad taught me. I still got that itch of excitement on game days, but with almost everything familiar about my early base-ball days taken away, it was less fun.

Our team did lousy that summer—four wins, sixteen losses. I wasn't used to that kind of record after playing for the champion Astros. I reached out to Mr. Gallo and others to help me through this dry year. The only highlight that summer was that I was picked for the all-star team, an honor that went to few 13-year-olds.

Throughout junior high, sports still occupied most of my waking thoughts. One day, I was surprised to find myself thinking about girls, too.

From the beginning, I was a one-woman kind of guy. Like most boys my age, when I was attracted to a girl, I was unable to tell her. I wrote notes and sent messages through others. Getting her phone number—well that set off a whole new set of nerves. My stomach did flip-flops before dialing her number the first time. Having a girlfriend was a whole new ballgame.

By the time I moved on to ninth grade, I was in the jock clique.

That status was important to me and made everything—socially, academically, and sports-wise—seem a little more serious and adult-like.

I became more motivated about schoolwork. It became a new form of competition. Getting better grades and comparing them to others was like trying to outdo rival teammates for batting averages and RBIs. Making the honor roll boosted my ego in the same way as getting my name in the newspaper for hitting a "dinger."

I wasn't the skinny kid anymore, either. I grew some and put on weight, though not enough to concern me or anyone else. I was eating a lot more than before. I especially liked pizza, hamburgers, and my all-time favorites—mashed potatoes and french fries. Dad had told me to eat more potatoes, right? Thank God for the metabolism of youth. Since Dad wasn't there to make me, and Mom didn't push, I was less likely to "eat the veggies" or "finish the lima beans" before going out to play.

To most outsiders, my life seemed just fine. It wasn't.

I didn't listen to Mom like I had Dad. I was "one of the men of the house" now. I started making up my own rules. I stayed out late, went places without asking permission, and left homework until the last minute. As a youngster, I thought getting away with these things was cool.

While most kids my age fought their parents' efforts to shape and control their behavior, I got little to no resistance at all from Mom. I could almost do whatever I wanted. Our rules were lax to non-existent.

Don't get me wrong. She loved us and gave us 150 percent of what she was able. The hand she was dealt wasn't fair. Raising four children on a policeman's pension and Social Security was not an easy task. Even though my dad's mom, "NaNa," lived with us, and my mom's parents moved close by, we were a handful. Little did I know then how this lack of structure and discipline would have a major effect on my adult life.

Others noticed what was going on, though. One of them was Frank Mazzei, my dad's friend, who coached my Pony and Legion league teams. At one point, when I was about 14, he and his wife, Marcia, even considered adopting me because they were worried about my welfare.

The Mazzeis found themselves in a moral dilemma. They felt I needed more structure than I was getting at home, but they didn't know how to adopt me without hurting my mom. There were three other kids to consider, too. In the end, the Mazzeis did their best to provide me with a place I always felt comfortable and the influence of a stable home. My other "surrogate" fathers, many of them friends of Mom and Dad, also tried to guide me as best they could.

Some of Dad's old-school lessons stuck with me. Once he locked me in a jail cell at the police station, hoping to scare me so I never wanted to end up behind bars. As loose as my boundaries were, I managed to stay out of trouble throughout my adolescence. Same with smoking. Dad once stuck a cigar in my mouth and made me smoke it until I got sick. I have never smoked, though I'm not sure whether it was because of his lesson or because I knew smoking helped kill him. I avoided the drug scene, too.

The one lesson that Dad never had the chance to teach me was the "birds and the bees." Until I finally figured things out in high school, I had some serious misconceptions about even the basics. If Dad had ever given Lee a man-to-man talk, my brother never shared it with me. And I never bothered asking. Instead, I relied on the vague information presented in sex education classes and misinformation of peers.

Much as Mom was unable to be a disciplinarian, when it came to her kids, she was fiercely loyal and unselfish.

One of the highlights of my life happened while doing a tenth-grade health project. My teacher, Bob Ford, assigned us a "home improvement project" to create a safer home environment. Some students put fire exit signs on the walls and others designed emergency escape procedures. My idea was to get Nelda Adams to stop smoking.

Mom was never a heavy smoker, maybe one to five cigarettes a day. I didn't care how much she smoked. I just knew I wanted her to stop. Dad had been a smoker—and he was gone.

Guilt didn't work. Flushing cigarettes down the toilet didn't work. Quoting statistics didn't work. I gave up.

We had to turn in a report explaining the steps we had taken to accomplish the project. A parent had to sign the report to confirm our efforts. Near the end of the page-and-a-half report, I wrote that trying to get Mom to stop smoking was worth the time, but I had "failed" in my attempt.

The way Mom read the paper, she thought I was going to fail health class because of her smoking. From the moment she signed the paper, Mom never smoked another cigarette. Through the years, I've never doubted the depth of the love she has for each of her children, and especially me.

As a sophomore, my sports abilities blossomed. Sometimes, Coach Misenhelter would ask me and another tenth grader, Mike Christ, to dress for varsity basketball games.

My moment of glory came that year during the second round of the WPIAL (Western Pennsylvania Interscholastic Athletic League) playoff games at the Civic Arena in Pittsburgh. As the final buzzer sounded, I scored. Penn Hills lost the game to Uniontown but the gamblers loved me. Because of the final point spread, many hometown folks won the bets they'd placed with the local bookies.

Most of the discipline and structure in my life came from participating in team sports, especially the American Legion team coached by my surrogate dads, Bill Deem Jr., Bill Deem Sr., Frank Mazzei, and Len Gallo. They knew the sport, and taught us how to win and lose with class. Most importantly, they taught me how to be a man.

My first Legion game was the best in all my sixteen years. I remember Coach Deem telling me, "You keep hitting like this, young man, and we're going to have some fun." Coach Mazzei recalls that some teams made "Eddie Adams rules," changing the ground rules in right field to prevent me from hitting home runs. I played well that whole season, hitting some long home runs in the playoffs that caught the attention of Major League scouts. I was on a roll.

Ed was also a talented basketball player at Penn
Hills High School.

I was on a roll with my eating habits, too. Just before basketball
season my junior year, someone pointed out to me that I could stand to
lose a couple pounds.

Me? The skinny kid? Lose weight? No way!

They were right. The extra potatoes, pizzas, and hamburgers finally
caught up with me, adding about ten or fifteen extra pounds. My friend
and "personal trainer," Nick Vacco, helped me lose the weight by
encouraging me to stick to a protein-only diet. The good part was I
could eat all the meat I wanted. The downside was that I missed my
pizzas and taters.

This began a yearly cycle—losing weight in the fall, keeping it off for basketball and baseball seasons, then gaining it back, plus some, in the summer. I maintained the loss easier during basketball because the sport was more physically taxing than baseball, when the weight started creeping back.

By my senior year, I had 15 to 20 pounds to lose. The weight threatened my agility and my identity. I loved sports. But I also had a growing love for food.

I liked the accomplishment of losing weight, but I didn't like depriving myself of my favorite foods. Dieting made me moody and irritable. I was used to satisfying the urge to eat whenever I damn well pleased. I developed a yearning for food. What I didn't understand then was the yearning was really a way of filling the hole in my soul left by my dad's death.

Junior year, I found someone to help fill the void. Her name was Chris Aquiline. She was a cheerleader who caught my eye as she sold Penn Hills High Football megaphones in the stands at a game. Short blonde hair. Nice legs. Laughing. Cute in her uniform.

I bought her last megaphone. I had to get to know her better.

I found reasons to talk to her in the halls at school or at football games. I got her phone number. I grew more excited each time I saw her. After a month or so, I asked her out. Soon after, we were going steady. Ed, the jock, dating Chris, the cheerleader. What could be more perfect? Chris and I did everything together—and we fell in love. I spent a lot of time getting to know her family. We often dropped in at the Mazzeis to play games or just hang out. She came to many of my games and was very supportive. I liked having her there and wanted to make her proud.

The good performance that began for me in Legion baseball after my sophomore year continued my junior year. I hit .625 that season. My name was all over the newspapers. People began talking Major League ball. I got a rush from having scouts coming to see me play.

They were watching others, too. Our talented team had seven players who went on to college or minor league teams. One of them was Tony Lonero, who, after playing for Louisiana State University, became a professional player in Italy and was a member of the 1982 Italian Olympic baseball team.

At first, I saw Tony as a threat. Baseball was my turf—at least in Penn Hills. Tony was every bit as good as I was or maybe better. From that rivalry grew a great friendship that has lasted through today. Tony has the rare gift of inspiring those around him to do better. His work ethic is contagious. I worked out more, practiced more, and no doubt became a better player because of Tony.

Senior year was my time to shine. Our baseball team won the WPIAL championships and placed second in the state. I was named WPIAL Baseball Player of the Year, a great honor.

Major League and college scouts talked to my coaches about my future in baseball. But I still didn't know whether I'd be attending college in the fall or be playing for a minor league team. If I went to the minors, there was a very real possibility it could lead to a Major League contract. At the Legion state championship games after my senior year, the coaches heard rumors that the Philadelphia Phillies were interested in me. But when it came to drafting players straight out of high school in the

Ed during his high school playing years.

late 1970s, the rules were a bit different than today. Coach Mazzei tells me that the Major League tended not to draft players who were going to college.

After the WPIAL championship game, a reporter from the Pittsburgh Post-Gazette inaccurately reported that I had accepted a full scholarship to the University of South Carolina. I had visited the school, but there had been no offers extended. That report may have cost me a chance at professional baseball.

Ironically, very soon after, the South Carolina Gamecocks did offer me a full scholarship. It was a chance to play for a NCAA Division I team that had ranked second in the nation the previous year—and get an education for free. I couldn't turn down the opportunity.

Before summer was over, Chris and I took our graduation money and traveled to Los Angeles to visit friends of her family. We had fun going to the "Tonight Show," touring Universal Studios, and catching rays on the beach. We grew even closer that summer.

I wanted Chris to come with me to South Carolina. Honestly, I wanted her to come with me more than anything on earth. She was extremely bright and had applied to Ivy League colleges like Harvard and Radcliffe. I knew that the University of South Carolina, while a decent school, couldn't offer her the quality of education she deserved. In the end, she decided to attend the prestigious Dickinson College in Carlisle, Pa.

We'd already been together two years and I had thoughts of us getting married after college. I felt we had a strong relationship, though I knew maintaining it with a 700-mile separation would be hard. I told myself that we could survive the four years apart. People kept telling me that if it were meant to be, we'd still be together.

I wanted desperately to believe them.

5

GOING TO CAROLINA

An empty, lifeless shoebox made of bricks, painted an institutional off-white. This was my home at the University of South Carolina, an eighth-floor dorm room in Bates House. The high-rise dorm was a five-minute walk to the ballfield in one direction, a ten-minute walk to the campus in the other.

I arrived before my roommate, Paul Hollins, a freshman ballplayer from New York. Most of the ballplayers lived in The Roost, the dorm that overlooked the baseball diamond. I remember feeling a bit separated from the athletes and the camaraderie the sports-connected Roost offered.

I decorated the wall with many sports posters, a Farrah Fawcett poster, and other things from home. But in a few weeks, as homesickness set in, I realized that home was in Penn Hills and my heart was with Chris, 700 miles away. I was lonely for a long while. Although I was outgoing and confident in my athletic abilities, I was not as sure of myself socially and academically.

The first several weekends, I stayed in my dorm room watching "Love Boat" on the nine-inch, black-and-white TV I'd brought from home. When I wasn't absorbed in a show, I replayed scenes from home in my mind and how I'd rather be there.

Except for Mom, my family didn't make much of a fuss about me leaving. But that was their way. Chris' mom, and a few of her brothers and sisters, drove us to Pittsburgh International Airport so she could say a final goodbye before I left. I had conflicting emotions as we drove along the highway in their light green GMC van. I held Chris' hand. I was sad to be leaving her, my family, and the town I called home. On the other hand, I was excited to be playing NCAA Division I college baseball for one of the best teams in the nation.

It was a lot for an eighteen-year-old to handle.

High school and sports had brought some stability to my life after dad died. Now I was headed for big changes yet again. My thoughts focused mostly on baseball. It made things bearable.

It took a while before I felt comfortable, even with baseball. New teammates. New fields. Different uniforms. Tougher competition. For the first time in my life, I wasn't "23," the number I had claimed since Little League days through high school and Legion play. Now I was "26."

Playing in the South was so different from Pittsburgh. We were confined indoors for only a short time during winter. The rest of the year, we played outside. At Carolina, the first game was in late February. Up North, we were lucky if games started by late April.

The extra playing was just fine with me.

Division I baseball at Carolina was similar to Major League ball in other cities since Columbia, S.C. had no Major League team. The college athletic teams were treated like pro teams. The local press covered everything. Autograph seekers approached us ballplayers on the street, especially after we had a good game. I felt important.

Because the USC Gamecocks finished second in the country in 1977, national attention focused on our team. Randy Martz, the 1977 college player of the year, and Mookie Wilson, who had a good Major League career with the New York Mets, both had just graduated. This could be the ticket to the Major Leagues and I felt lucky to have the chance.

Despite all the drama of being away from home, my first year at

Carolina went well. My grades were a little lower than the B-plus average I maintained in high school, but I did well at baseball, especially given my freshman status.

When I wasn't in class, studying, practicing, playing, or partying, I was on the phone, trying to bring Penn Hills and Chris closer through the wires. I logged a few $100-plus phone bills that year. Each week, when the local newspaper arrived by mail, I'd devour every article. I was homesick—very homesick.

I did make friends with teammates and in the co-ed dorm. But unlike many of the other guys, I wasn't out to score with the girls. I never was a player. I was a one-woman man and Chris was that woman. So, my socializing didn't include dating or trying to have sex.

One thing that helped with the loneliness was USC's Penn Hills connection. Three of Penn Hills' best football players had scholarships there—Lou Biondi; Mike Fralic, whose brother Bill went on to play for the Atlanta Falcons and Detroit Lions; and Len Gallo, Jr., my "surrogate" brother. When Mr. Gallo came to see Len, Jr. play, he made a point of stopping to see me, too.

But the highlight of my year was when Chris agreed to spend her spring break with me. I'd sent her money so she could make the trip south by car with some friends headed to spring break in Florida. We planned to meet along I-95, the highway south from Pennsylvania. I almost didn't make it. The friend driving me to meet Chris was pulled over for speeding and had to pay the fine on the spot. Fortunately, between everyone in the car, we scraped up the $20 necessary.

As excited as I was to see her, it took a little while to get reacquainted after being apart for a few months.

Our first full day together was one of my best days at Carolina. The Gamecocks played Southern Illinois that day and I hit a home run. I made the local sports news on television that night. I was so proud—and so happy that Chris was there to share the moment with me. I was on cloud nine.

But as the evening ended, my world came crashing in yet again. We had gone out partying and I was drunk by the time we returned to the dorm room. Out of the blue, Chris informed me that she wanted to "see other people." I raised hell. Loud enough that it seemed the whole dorm had come to my room to see what the commotion was about.

"Get her the #@%&! out of here," I told my friends. "Send her back on the bus."

Fortunately for everyone, I passed out.

Chris ended up staying the week as planned. We managed to have a good time, and though I tried getting us back to the way we were, these were our last few days together. I tried hard to get her to change her mind. She didn't.

Losing Chris reopened the wounds of losing Dad. I felt lost without her.

I came home for the summer and worked at the local Boys' Club, coaching and running athletic programs. I also played sandlot baseball for Swissvale in the Greater Pittsburgh Federation League. Like other years, I gained some weight, then had to lose it for fall baseball.

When I returned to college that fall, I didn't actively seek out a girlfriend. I was shy when it came to relationships and I didn't like the idea of sleeping around, as some guys did. I dated a little bit. But baseball continued to be my focus.

I had high hopes for my sophomore year. They ended over Christmas break 1978.

While home for the holidays, my high school teammate Tony Lonero and I went to work out at a racquetball club in nearby Monroeville. During a game, I jumped as high as I could to hit the ball, and all of my weight came down on my left ankle as it twisted. I waited a week to seek treatment because the medical care was free at school.

The doctor there put me in a cast. I didn't break the ankle, but the doctor told me it would have been better if I had. Ligament damage took longer to heal and I needed rehabilitation. I was red-shirted for the spring ball season. Not playing baseball was the last straw.

Homesickness, losing Chris, and now baseball was threatened. That is when I began self-destructing. Something inside me snapped.

I began secretive and bizarre eating habits, like taking my gym bag to the cafeteria, filling it with food, then back to my dorm to eat later. I'd order a pizza and eat it somewhere no one else could see me or have any. I'd eat big meals out in restaurants and pay by writing bad checks or running out on the bill.

Friday night partying extended into Thursday nights. Then Wednesdays. I started blowing off classes and my grades fell. I was still dressing at home games but did not travel with the team. The coach noticed the difference in my appearance and began daily weigh-ins in an effort to make me lose weight.

I'd been through the routine of losing weight before. I knew how to do it. But for some reason when I went to the track to run, I didn't have the whiff to do it. I was in the middle of living my dream, and I was shutting down.

On the way back from a pre-season game, we stopped at a restaurant buffet. I came back to the table with a large dessert. Right there, in front of all my teammates, Coach June Raines told me bluntly, "That's what's keeping you off the field."

I went to the parking lot, looked at the sky and cried, "Why can't I stop!"

I just couldn't.

I began pulling away from everything and everybody. I called home less. Coach Mazzei kept in touch with Coach Raines and knew I was in trouble. Coach Mazzei called me a few times, trying to help straighten me out, but to no avail. If he had been my dad, he told me later, he could have "grabbed me by the throat and said, 'get to class.'" Frank Mazzei was a major influence on my life. But he was right. He wasn't my dad.

I am convinced that if Dad had been alive, I would not have been in this downward spiral. If he had been alive, he would have helped me get over Chris. If he had been alive, I would have rebounded from my injury. If he had been alive, I wouldn't have been stuffing a hole in my heart with food.

I got the call in my dorm room. Coach Raines told me my scholarship was not being renewed. He had a team to run and there just wasn't room for someone who was screwing up and who wasn't doing his share.

The destruction was complete. The end of my college education. The end of my Major League dreams. Everything crumbled right before my eyes.

Food and partying won. Eddie Adams lost.

6

STRIKING OUT

The headlines that once proclaimed my talents might as well have announced my failure to the world— "Eddie Adams strikes out at Carolina"— though now I was yesterday's news and not worthy of even a sentence. I came home from Carolina ashamed, like a dog with his head down and his tail between his legs. I wanted to hide. When I couldn't, I tried to save face.

"That damn ankle," I told everyone.

The story went on that I never quite recovered from the injury on the racquetball court. The team needed someone who could play, so the coach had no choice but to take away the scholarship. The short, credible explanation deflected the blame. I began to believe my own lies.

The truth of what really happened there wasn't clear to me until many years later. I have no doubt now that this is when my eating addiction took root. If someone had said to me at age nineteen, "Ed, you're a food addict," I would have laughed. I wouldn't have cared. I didn't know the signs then. Ordering a pizza and hoarding it for myself. Financing a binge by writing bad checks at restaurants. Starting to party on Thursdays—then Wednesdays, Tuesdays and Mondays—because I couldn't wait for the weekend.

I was no longer hungry to be the best baseball player at any cost.

My appetite was for food and partying. The price I paid was high—my scholarship and my dream of being a professional ballplayer.

This new, unhealthy lifestyle began to control me. My life started a downward spiral, my weight an upward one. I gained twenty pounds in the first several weeks home.

By the time summer baseball rolled around, I was already 240 pounds. I was the catcher for Pittsburgh Federation League's sandlot team in Swissvale, a suburb near Penn Hills. I was still a good player, just slower running the bases and no longer on the verge of playing in the Major Leagues. Behind my back, my teammates had dubbed me "Michelin Man" because of my growing rolls of fat. By the end of the season, I was nearly sixty pounds heavier than my high school playing weight. Despite my worsening condition, I played a good game. I still loved hitting that baseball.

My life was nothing now but playing ball and bingeing. I quickly learned which bars served underage drinkers. I wouldn't turn twenty-one for nearly another year. For five dollars, I could give myself an "attitude adjustment." I felt sorry for myself. I had no job, no ambition, no motivation. I loafed for a whole year. Mom provided the shelter over my head and the all-important food.

There were occasional reminders of my baseball failure that I had to face. There were also reminders about my failed relationship with Chris. I held on to photos of her for years before finally throwing them out.

Eventually, a friend got me a job at a local Pizza Hut. Not the greatest place for a budding food addict to work.

In the span of a year and a half, I went from a promising Major League prospect to a 300-pound dishwasher. I gave lip service to making a comeback. But I gave mouth service to pizza, which had rapidly replaced baseball as the most important thing in my life. In my moments of clarity, I still didn't understand why.

The best thing that had happened to me since Carolina was when Pizza Hut sent me to management school. The respect helped build my crushed ego, and I took the job seriously and performed it with pride. But, in retrospect, a strange pattern had emerged. With each promotion, from dishwasher to line cook to assistant manager, my weight got "promoted," too. As I grew from 350 to 400 pounds, I sometimes wondered if my skin would explode.

On nights off, or if there was time after closing Pizza Hut, I made time to go to Bernie's Lounge, a bar where I was a regular. During high school, my friends Nick Vacco, Kirk Thompson, and I formed VAT (Vacco, Adams, Thompson) Disco Productions and deejayed two dances at school. It was something I had fun doing then. I had just purchased a new $500 Fisher stereo, so I convinced the owners at Bernie's to let me bring it in and play some music.

By chance, the day of the big show, I ran into my brother David's friend, a sometimes-disc jockey who loaned me some extra equipment and helped set it up. I loved doing it so much that within a week I had my own deejay equipment. Mr. Ed's Music Service was born.

At first, I played for drinks, then for $20 on top. The business began to flourish as I landed steady gigs at some local watering holes.

I was living a food addict's dream. I'd work at Pizza Hut during the day and eat free pizza. Then I'd spin records at night and get free drinks. It is no accident that my jobs allowed me to eat and drink all the time.

I thrived as a member of management at Pizza Hut and owning my own deejay business. But a full-time management schedule and playing up to fifteen deejay jobs a month was demanding. And I was beginning to worry about my future with Pizza Hut, even though I had been a good employee for five years.

I struggled to fit into the required manager's uniform—black pants and vest, button-down dress shirt, tie, and name tag. I ripped seams, blew out crotches, and popped buttons. Frequently, I'd excuse myself and head to the men's room with a stapler for a quick fix. I'd learned to sew out of necessity to repair the pants at home. Many times, I'd stay close to the register or the table where pizza was prepared just to hide the embarrassing holes. Often, I brought a second pair of pants. On a few occasions, I ripped them both. On top of my sloppy appearance, my hygiene began to slip as my weight made it more difficult to clean myself thoroughly.

The manager and area supervisor began to confront me about how I looked. To their credit, they never screamed at me for being heavy. I knew my job security was about as stable as my pant seams. Both were ready to bust soon.

Part of being an addict is lying. I wanted to get out of Pizza Hut before I was fired. Losing some weight and improving my appearance was hard work. I hated diets. Because the deejay business had grown to about twenty jobs a month, I was making more with that than working at the restaurant. I could avoid the whole mess by simply walking away. So, I did. Walking away was easy and the monster of an addict inside me could continue to be fed. I came up with another brilliant lie.

I told my supervisors and co-workers that I was quitting Pizza Hut to devote myself full-time to the deejay business. I explained that I had always wanted to own a business and that working both jobs left me tired all the time. And some of that was true.

Just like when I left Carolina, I bought into my own lie. The pretense enabled me to believe, on some twisted level, that I was moving forward with my life. The truth was that this addictive stroke of genius allowed me to keep overeating and drinking. I never considered myself to be an alcoholic but there was no question that I abused alcohol. It numbed me to the things that weren't right in my life. But it was food I craved, not a drink.

Despite the fact my health was worsening, Mr. Ed's Music Service was a success. At its peak, I was working six nights a week. Ironically, I played several Christmas parties for the local Pizza Huts.

I was often the life of the party and made new friends easily. Being the deejay was fun. I was the center of attention, got free drinks all the time, and ended most jobs by stopping at an all-night restaurant and devouring a big meal. If I weren't in the mood to eat out, I'd bring home a "binge in a bag" from the store. Having a hangover never mattered because the gigs never started until eight or nine the next night.

Saturdays were best. I did weddings on Saturdays and could make a week's salary from Pizza Hut in only four or five hours. The hours were earlier than bar work, so I was always done by eight or nine, leaving plenty of time to hit the bars with a pocketful of money and a ravenous appetite.

About the time I was twenty-seven, the reality hit me that this was the year of my ten-year high school reunion. I had always loved school. It had provided structure when my home life didn't. I had been one of the star athletes. I looked at myself now and knew I didn't want to show up looking as I did. I had tried diets and failed each time. Then Frank Mazzei offered what I considered to be an intriguing proposition. He suggested that I move in with him and his wife so that my food intake could be monitored. The arrangement with the Mazzeis didn't last, though. They caught me sneaking in food. Eventually I knew it was time to leave and move back in with my mom.

I did manage to get down to 300 pounds in time for the reunion. I also underwent a mini-reclamation project, visiting the dentist and buying myself new clothes. During this time, I began to date a girl named Jackie Rosenhoover. She had been the girlfriend of my brother's friend. What I liked about her was that she liked me for who I was, fat and all. I went overboard, leaving notes, gifts, and balloons on her parked car while she was at work. Best of all, she agreed to go to the reunion with me. Unfortunately, she and her ex-boyfriend decided to get back together before the reunion date. I was crushed. I invested too much emotional energy too quickly. The end of this short relationship hurt me badly. She offered to go to the reunion with me but I didn't feel right about it. So, I went by myself.

Fortunately, I'd volunteered to serve on the reunion committee and did a lot of the organizing. I was thankful I did because I was busy enough that night not to worry about how I looked or what people were saying about me—or about the fact that I was alone. Chris came and we talked for about forty-five minutes. It was a bittersweet conversation. It felt good to catch up with her but it reminded me of all the could-have-beens and should-have-beens. She was already married and our lives weren't destined to come together again. So, it was no Jackie, no Chris. After that night, my aloneness was just that much more pronounced.

Back to filling the void with food.

It didn't take long to reach 500 pounds. Though I had fun at the bars, the relationships in my life suffered. I didn't even remotely consider dating at that weight. I began isolating from my friends and places I liked to go because of a growing shame in myself. The extra pounds gave me an excuse, protected me from not getting hurt again.

Like many addicts, I gave the outward appearance that everything was fine. I smiled, laughed, told jokes, and was fun to be around. My secret thoughts were anything but upbeat.

Quietly, I suffered in my own private hell. I was a failure in my own eyes. I was an idiot for letting my life get out of hand. I was killing myself. And worst of all, I was alone. I wouldn't let anyone in to help and I couldn't help myself. A burgeoning depression kept me stuck and caused me not to care about it all. I sometimes wondered what people said when I left the room and whether my social interactions were largely artificial.

Among other ailments, I was having occasional chest pains and cramps in my side near the heart. One night on the way home from the bar, the chest pains and cramps hit at the same time. I thought I was having a heart attack. I made it home but was scared more than I ever remember being in my life. My reaction horrified my mom, who must have had thoughts of losing me, just as she had lost my dad. After forty-five minutes of physical and emotional terror, the pains finally passed. I wasn't even willing to call for help for myself, even though I would have called an ambulance for anyone else in the same predicament.

That night, I wrote a will. It wasn't because I had any money to speak of. It was mostly to apologize to my family. I was ashamed of what I'd become.

The insanity of it all is that I always come back to the food. The next night, I was out again, drinking and gorging myself to numb the intensity of the night before. I began having random thoughts about my mortality, even though I was still in my late twenties. But mostly I worried about what my next meal was going to be and how I could get it with the least amount of exertion and attention.

My brother David, who had been a pain-in-the-ass, get-in-trouble-all-the-time adolescent, began earning my deep respect as an adult. My family was obviously worried about me and although he was the youngest, David was the one who did the dirty work by confronting me about the worries they all had about my health.

He had heard about a program at St. Francis Medical Center in Pittsburgh for people with eating disorders. He was a private detective and had looked into all the details about how to be admitted for treatment. After explaining to me what he knew, he handed me a phone number.

I didn't know what was on the other side of that phone number. I just stared at it for three days. Thoughts went through my head. I was already thirty. I wanted a wife, a family, and all the things that come with them. I wanted to be healthy. I wanted to play ball again.

On the fourth day, I picked up the phone and dialed.

7

52 DAYS IN LOCKUP

I was scared, unsure of what was in store for me. I was thirty years old and fat —and it was my own idiotic fault. I also knew I needed help.

Thanks to the groundwork laid by David, I was able to make all the arrangements. Now all I had to do was show up at the emergency room of St. Francis on March 12, 1990 to check myself in.

As I rode to the hospital with mom and David that cool morning, I had in my head that I was just going to get help for an eating problem. I didn't realize at the time how wrong I was.

After filling out some paperwork, I was taken to a room and searched for things they didn't allow in the hospital—things like sharp objects and food. I've never felt so violated. It became clear to me that I was going to be locked up not just in a hospital, but a psychiatric hospital. Words like "loony bin" and "wacko ward" ran through my head. I was nervous as hell.

Because I was not the only admission that day, I had to wait . . . and wait. I grew antsy as I watched the waiting room TV with mom and David. After a while, I told them they didn't have to stay with me, so they left. I passed another anxious hour alone.

I was offered a lunch tray. A short time later, one of the Eating

Disorders Unit nurses finally came for me. I struggled to walk to the unit, trying hard to catch my breath as I tried to keep up with her.

The Eating Disorders Unit was an odd mix of twenty patients suffering from anorexia, bulimia, or compulsive overeating. Some of the anorexics were on bed rest until they were strong enough to sit up. From my perspective, it was inconceivable that anyone could deny themselves food. Most of the patients were obese, like me.

Walking the unit halls was eerie, like walking into a new job or classroom. After getting very heavy, I'd avoided places with new people, so being on the unit made me self-conscious and nervous. My mood wasn't helped when the nurse showed me my room, which had a "lovely" view of historic Allegheny Cemetery.

It was lunchtime, so she took me to the common eating area. I chuckled to myself because, even though I had been at the hospital for only a few hours, I'd already been offered two trays of food.

After eating, I went through the admissions process with a nurse, who answered my many questions, and reviewed the rules and policies. She took my vital signs. I weighed in at 557 pounds. When she finished, I realized that whatever this treatment thing was, it was about to start.

I was assigned to Dr. Lore Rubin, who, with Dr. Ruth Kane, a noted eating disorders expert, was one of the two psychiatrists charged with overseeing my case and making the important decisions. A case nurse was assigned to get to know me and check with me occasionally about how I was doing with my treatment plan. I also had contact with a social worker, who ran the therapy group; a dietitian; physical and occupational therapists; and a number of doctors, nurses, aides, and receptionists.

The treatment team, as they called it, met weekly to decide on a course of action for me. They began by taking my history, learning as much as they could about me so they could better treat me. This was the first time I had admit a lot about myself and my problems to total strangers. I laid it all out—the failed diet attempts, gaining more than 300 pounds in ten years, bingeing at night, drinking to excess a few times a week, being unable to work because of my size and physical condition. I had passive thoughts about dying and, in moments of clarity, realized I was slowly committing suicide by overeating.

There were also things I didn't admit to them but, to my chagrin, they learned anyhow. My darkest secrets—like having to use a small plastic tub because I was not physically able to use a toilet and not wiping myself because I couldn't reach. I didn't tell them how irritated my skin was where the folds of fat prevented air from reaching the crevices.

I was absolutely humiliated when, fifteen days into my stay, a nurse named Don was assigned to wash me. I had to help him lift the flaps of flab to clean areas that were inaccessible to me. He found my skin irritated and broken open in many places and also a fungal infection. After he washed me, the odor was gone and he applied a soothing cream to help my skin heal. Staff members continued to treat my skin daily for a good part of my stay.

My diagnosis was a bit more than just an eating disorder. I was labeled as morbidly obese, meaning I was more than 100 pounds overweight. I was told I was a compulsive overeater, mildly depressed, and suffering from hypertension and shortness of breath. I was diagnosed with both dependent personality disorder and co-dependency.

Simply put, dependent personality disorder is characterized by an extreme need of other people and inability to be independent, marked by a fear of separation and rejection, indecisiveness, lack of self-confidence, and belittling oneself.

Codependency, on the other hand, propels a person into a search for a person, place, or thing to make him happy and fulfill his needs; provide him with a sense of self and to nurture an abandoned "inner child." This frequently leads a person to addictions, which are used to numb the pain. A codependent person often is his own best critic, and continues to seek the love and nurturing he feels he lacks.

I could see myself in both diagnoses.

In addition, after undergoing the standard battery of psychological tests, they determined I was "emotional empty"—meaning that I tended to avoid emotion and not be able to explain my feelings or experiences in any detail.

The team members noted I exhibited a certain defiance, like wearing improperly-fitting "flip flops" during the winter, even after they told me it would hurt my body to do so, and not using the sponges and other things they'd given me to help me clean myself.

My treatment included individual and group therapy. In these sessions, I began to learn what was wrong with me and how to begin recovery. Early in therapy, it became clear to the social worker, Claudia Warner, and me that my dad's death, the loss of my scholarship, and end of my dream to be a Major League Baseball player left me with an "emotional hunger." I was using food as an "anesthetic" to numb my pain. I didn't know why food made me feel better, but it did. Part of my problem seemed to stem from the fact that after dad died, mom was only able to take functional care of the family. Although she loved us deeply, she could not provide much emotional nurturing for us four kids. Without dad, there was no discipline or structure in our home, something that I evidently needed to develop normally.

Though I didn't like being locked up, I felt protected at St. Francis. The controlled environment gave me the structure that I'd been lacking for nearly two decades. The people there knew my problem. I didn't have to play games like hiding from others, as I did on the "outside," because I didn't feel as self-conscious. The patients on the unit were treated with respect.

I had a major "ah-ha" moment early in my stay. During a group session dealing with food addiction, Dorothy Lippmann, a psychiatric nurse, explained eating problems from a medical perspective.

"You have an addiction when it comes to your eating habits, and it's an illness."

She had my full attention.

"It's nobody's fault when they get an illness. If a person with cancer was in this very room, you wouldn't say to that person, 'Why do you have that illness and why don't you get rid of it?' You have an illness. It's not your fault that you have it. But it is your responsibility to get well from it."

I finally learned what was wrong with me. That knowledge lifted a large burden. I'd always wondered why I got so out of control.

All the laughs and snickers, all the rude comments, all the unpleasant social situations, all the broken furniture I'd endured. I carried several years of guilt into that hospital with me—guilt fueled by the inner voice that took me to task for being such a failure.

I was conditioned for many years to feel subhuman. It was a life-changing moment for me to hear I had an illness. Though the guilt and shame lingered, and lingers somewhat to this day, much of it washed away that day in therapy.

I never stopped and said, "Gee, this emotional pain is really getting to me. I think I'll eat a cake." It's just the way I dealt with things. I now understood why diets never worked for me. Taking away the food exposed why I could stand it for a while, but always ended up going back to food, the one thing in my life I could depend upon.

These people had my attention now. I wanted to know more. I immersed myself in my treatment.

Sticking with the food plan was actually the easiest part of my program. Even though I'd heard stories of people smuggling food in, there wasn't any chance for me to overeat. I was given a 1,200-calorie-a-day, low-salt diet that met dietary guidelines. In addition to nutritional supervision, I was educated about healthy eating, such as choosing wheat bread over white and avoiding sugar because of its addictive qualities.

I received treatment for the skills required for everyday living that I could not perform because of my weight. I learned proper hygiene habits and was given special tools to help make it easier to dress. There was recreational therapy for exercise, occupational therapy to help me live a better life, and art therapy to let out some of my emotional needs. I began walking the halls by myself for exercise once it was okayed by the medical team.

But the most important help I received was going to individual and group therapy, and attending the twelve-step program offered at the hospital. Claudia, who ran the group and handled my individual therapy, was particularly helpful in the process.

Working with her, I was able to express for the first time in nearly twenty years the mixture of anger and resentment I felt toward my mom.

After dad died, I didn't feel right getting mad at mom. Life handed her a rotten deal, taking away her husband and leaving her with four kids to raise on her own. In my mind, when dad died, I not only lost him, but my mother's affection as well. She just had little left to give us after coping with dad's death and, in fact, I found myself in the role of surrogate husband to her. I resented it. Now, although I was a grown man, I still wanted Mom to fulfill the role she was not able to play out after dad's death. Deep down, I wanted her to be a "mom" to me, but I also wanted her to be my father. Claudia felt there was a part of me that was upset that Mom wasn't Dad, that he had died and not her. As my weight climbed and I became more physically limited, I grew more and more dependent on Mom, as if I were a child. If being morbidly obese had a plus side, it was giving me the nurturing from Mom I had craved since I was twelve.

Claudia explained that by having Mom take care of me at my heaviest, I had become stuck in a four-year-old behavior, including having her clean up for me after toileting. The term for this pattern was "arrested development." I had some other "stuck" behaviors, too. Once I lost the scholarship, I couldn't get on with my life. My employment history was not equivalent with what I was capable of in terms of a career.

Though therapy, I learned that my inability to relate to women in a romantic way stemmed from my inability to think of myself as a grown-up man. It was another reason I continued to fill my emotional void with food. I might not have someone to hold me, but food never said no.

That problem with intimacy even surfaced during an encounter with Claudia when my paternal grandmother died during my stay. I had developed a crush on Claudia, something not that uncommon between patient and therapist. I was lying on the bed in my room, staring out at the cemetery after learning of my grandmother's death. Claudia came in to offer a comforting hug, but I never turned around, rejecting what I needed. I was unable to accept this simple act of consolation. It was something we discussed later in therapy.

Transference is the psychological term for transferring some trait from your relationship with your parent to another person. During therapy with Claudia, I was able to work out some of the issues I had with my mother, including separating from her and living my own life. I also learned that I had no control over my mother's happiness.

Eventually, the family came for a group session with me. It was the first time Lee, Jody, David, Mom, and I had ever discussed dad's death as a family. The session opened some doors with my loved ones that had been closed for too many years.

Identifying and admitting the problem was the first step in my recovery. The common thread I've seen with everyone I know in recovery from food addiction is that the psychological issues are dealt with along with the eating disorder. I learned that those who attempt to shortcut the process and only enjoy the physical recovery will inevitably relapse.

In my opinion, recovery is judged by society according to how much weight is lost. If emotional recovery were assigned a number, it would surpass the weight loss numbers by far. I found that reversing life-long, low self-esteem, emotional abuse, and beginning to let go of bottled up anger provides relief that far surpasses any amount of weight loss.

I was fortunate that my stay was covered by Medical Assistance. Unfortunately, health care programs today would not cover the cost of the intensive treatment I received.

After fifty-two days, I was ready to face the world again. I had lost eighty-eight pounds during my stay and I felt more hopeful than I had in years. I agreed to continue with a partial hospitalization program that would provide me with outpatient services on a daily basis for the next year.

I left through the same doors I'd entered. But I was not the same person, inside or out.

8

MR. RECOVERY

W ell, I made the All-Star Recovery Team. Of course, there wasn't one, but if there had been one, I would have been the star among the all-stars.

I wasn't content just to be a recovery superstar by weight-loss numbers alone. I wanted the recognition that came with success. And I made sure I got it—guest roles on a syndicated Christian television show and a local public television documentary, as well as establishing myself as a motivational speaker for local support groups.

I went at recovery the same way I'd gone at food—full bore, no holds barred. In fact, most of my waking hours were spent on recovery.

My fifty-two days in lockup gave me confidence, which was bolstered by the continued support of the partial hospitalization program for eating disorders at St. Francis Hospital. The program ran five days a week, like a school, and I continued to learn more about myself, eating addiction, and recovery. I'd lost a total of eighty-eight pounds in lockup and was determined to keep the number climbing.

My recovery was multi-faceted. I did the "90-90" program (ninety meetings in ninety days) with a twelve-step eating support group. Through those meetings, I made new friends, people like me—food addicts trying to control their compulsive eating problems. Step two of any twelve-step program, whether Alcoholics Anonymous, Narcotics Anonymous, or Overeaters Anonymous, is to come to believe that a power greater than ourselves can restore us to sanity. It involves a willingness to believe that a force or power greater than you will give you the strength to overcome the addiction.

This step is scary for many people working the program, whether devoutly religious, not religious at all, or just plain not sure, like I was. In the beginning, I found the power in the group itself. But as I grew, so did my belief that my help would come from my Savior, my God.

I found a faith community where I felt at home—Hebron Church in my hometown of Penn Hills. I delved into my newfound spirituality, eager to learn all I could about the Lord who had saved me from myself. I embraced Bible studies and finally began to receive the religious education I'd missed as a child. I became a deacon at the church, reaffirming my growing faith through the acknowledgement by my Hebron family that I was indeed worthy in the eyes of God to serve Him through His church.

It felt weird coming back to my home environment armed with the tools I received during treatment. I felt like I finally discovered what was wrong with me. I blamed myself less. My soul was restored through what might be the most important tool of all.

Hope.

The void I'd filled with food was now filled with a food plan, emotional support, exercise, spiritual support, and the love of God. The weight poured off me.

I adhered to the food plan in the same way I'd practiced obsessively to be the best basketball and baseball player. My whole eating pattern changed. I cut out sugars whenever possible, ate wheat bread instead of white, fixed salads for myself, and chose healthy meats.

I was so determined to make this work that on a trip to Clearwater, Fla. with the softball team that I coached, I passed on a large hotel breakfast for Grape Nuts in my room at 7 a.m. On another softball trip to York, Pa., I took a microwave oven so I could prepare my own food.

It all paid off. In just fourteen months, I had lost 314 pounds, dropping from 557 to 242. With my six-foot-tall frame, I was back in a healthy, normal range for the first time since college. I had surgery to remove the drapes of skin that hung off my body—and though I endured several drains as I healed and was left with life-long scars, the end result was definitely worth it. At age thirty-two, I had the world in front of me once again.

Life was wonderful. And I lived happily ever after.

Not!

The program I set up was working. Sometimes it was actually fun, like when I rode the stationary bike until a puddle of sweat formed on the floor below me. Other times, it was hard work, especially when I was tempted to stray from my food plan. Sticking with a food plan becomes tedious and monotonous at times. I wanted to run away from it. The knowledge that I was only one bite away from slipping into relapse left me feeling very vulnerable.

For a true addict, recovery can never be totally pushed to the side. Unfortunately, I proved again that I am a true addict.

As I began to pick my life back up, recovery was no longer every waking thought. My problem was I tried to leave recovery behind. I always learn the hard way.

There were a few turning points, in retrospect, that doomed my success.

The first came after I finished the outpatient treatment. I decided to return to college and study liberal arts at Community College of Allegheny County-Boyce Campus. I went at my studies full steam ahead, as with everything I do. As school became my main focus, I started watering down the things I had begun doing in recovery. It got to the point that I was hardly paying any attention to the very things that kept the food addict inside at bay.

I had a new drive—to be a straight-A student. I started playing baseball for the college team as well as the JV Lounge men's softball team with my buds. This time, I was not going to be sent away from the game. I would quit on my terms. I even started dating a little.

After ten years of being imprisoned by my fat, I was living life again. What did I need recovery for? The reality was I had developed a false sense of being able to do things I shouldn't, things that would start packing the pounds back on.

Like I said, I learn the hard way.

A second turning point came at a softball tournament in Clearwater, Fla. My teammates and I were enjoying the games and the vacation-like atmosphere. Food was part of the moment, just like it had been back in the days of the Astros when my dad was alive.

It was a bag of potato chips that started a drip of what was to become a flood of relapse. I was in the gift shop of the Holiday Inn where we stayed, getting a diet soda, when I noticed a bag of Lay's potato chips that were burnt on purpose and sold that way for people who liked the burnt ones. I thought I'd buy them, just to show the guys. Surely, they would laugh that someone would buy a bag of burnt chips.

It was not the epiphany I thought it would be, but in the end, I had a ten-ounce bag of chips in my possession. I opened them to see what the burnt chips looked like and tasting one wouldn't hurt anything, so I ate one. I figured that since I did not become a raving-craving maniac having eaten something off my food plan, that I could finish the bag, which I did.

I had given the addiction monster life. No warning bells went off. No one slapped my hand. Three hundred pounds didn't land on me in punishment. But those few chips fed a sleeping beast. The addict inside awakened. He shook the dust off his shoulders, raised his head, and spoke.

"Hey, I can eat this stuff again!"

The relapse started with little permissions. A bag of chips here. A piece of cake there. Then came the medium permissions. One piece of pizza. Ah, c'mon. Two won't hurt. The portions I ate of the permissible foods got gradually bigger because I began not measuring.

My guard was down. I was ripe for a total relapse.

The necessary wall built by nearly two years of recovery came crashing down. The tools I needed to fight back were buried in the rubble. Without them, I was no match for the addict within. Food was my God again, and that is a disease of the spirit.

The weight came back little by little. The hole I get stuck in was being dug again. I was digging it myself.

On the surface, life was going well.

After excelling both academically and socially at CCAC-Boyce, I enrolled as a sociology major at Indiana University of Pennsylvania. At IUP, I continued counseling with Corrine Zupanik. But it wasn't enough to keep me on the straight and narrow. I came home on weekends to deejay because I needed money. I stayed in the home of Betty McGuire, a friend whom I'd met at Boyce. Although I was relapsing, I appeared on a show, set in a diner, that was filmed at a local Christian station to discuss my weight loss. A part of me felt like a liar.

As the weight came back, dating was pushed aside. My sexuality has always been an underlying issue. Intimacy with a woman intimidates me. When opportunities presented themselves, I either chickened out or shut down. Then I'd move away from the person, left with another notch of self-worthlessness in my belt.

By July 1994, with a bachelor's degree in hand and graduate school at the University of Pittsburgh just ahead, I was totally out of control. I was suffering from a major bout of depression brought on by my total relapse. Although I was only 35, I had severe arthritis in my left ankle and knee. And I had a bigger problem.

I couldn't stop eating.

I looked at myself in the mirror. In some ways, I viewed the regained weight as a welcomed visitor. There were parts of my life that were more comfortable with the buffer of added pounds. As much as a part of me wanted a serious relationship with a woman, the added weight kept me safe from intimacy.

I turned to St. Francis Hospital again, hoping that hospitalization could give me a jump start in regaining control. This time, I was locked up for only 19 days, enough time for me to get back on track. But recovery was short-lived, lasting only one month.

I was living on my own in a subsidized apartment complex in Monroeville. While it enabled me to have a life separate from my mother, one of the goals of my first hospitalization, it also left me alone to indulge my addiction with no one around to see. I also began pulling away from the church and my God—again.

The real Ed continued to shine on the surface. I did extremely well in my master of social work program at the University of Pittsburgh. But when I left the classroom or part-time deejay job, the addict took over my life, dragging me down into that abyss of loneliness and hopelessness.

In December 1995, I was hospitalized a third time, spending several days of the Christmas holiday away from my family. Fortunately, I got a Christmas Day pass so I didn't spend the day alone in lockup. Binge eating and depression had thrown me into a 450-pound hole. Being buried there put me into a deep funk for about six months, leaving me powerless to claw my way up and out.

Again, the support of the St. Francis program gave me the strength to fight.

I finished school in 1996 and was hired that fall by CCAC as a part-time sociology instructor. I was comfortable within Boyce Campus' familiar halls, comfortable enough to forget about my growing girth from time to time.

I took on the job as commissioner of a summer men's softball league.

I have always been blessed with a wonderful support system of family and friends. But they weren't enough. I longed for the lives my siblings had—a home, marriage, kids.

As my condition continued to decline, I decided to move in with my mom once again. We settled in a small, two-bedroom frame house along one of Penn Hills' busiest streets. It was a food addict's dream come true. Within sight, there were a number of fast food joints, restaurants, and a large supermarket. Drive-throughs made it all so easy; I never had to leave the car. So did ordering food through the Internet. Cookies, chocolates, nuts, cakes and groceries—all delivered to my doorstep without the embarrassment of shopping for food and being seen in public.

Eventually, though, I'd have the moment of clarity that lit my flame of willpower. Usually, it was as I hit another low.

I returned to St. Francis for the final time in September 1999. I weighed in at 686 pounds. The doctors diagnosed me with depression, breathing problems, high blood pressure, arthritis, insomnia, and sleep apnea, not to mention my eating disorder. I only stayed five days this time. I was forty years old and a mess.

This time, it wasn't just that I wanted to lose weight or wanted a stab at dating or playing ball again.

I was very afraid of dying—the most afraid I've ever been in my life.

I went home again. Part of me had a passive death wish. The other part, a hope of fighting. As an athlete, I always gave it my all. The soul of an athlete hidden under all those rolls of flab started a tug of war with the addict.

9

BOTTOM OF THE NINTH

The dream replayed often in my mind. I'd wear a black-and-gold Pittsburgh Pirates uniform. I'd feel the excitement of the young fans who would yell my name as I warmed up. I'd hit a home run into the stands at Three Rivers Stadium in front of a hometown crowd. From the stands, my wife and kids would watch me trot around the bases. Food addiction killed those dreams. And now it was killing me.

I was dying a gradual death—dying to eat.

From my sophomore year in college until I was forty-one, my life was controlled by the overconsumption of food. Honestly, I reached a point where I just didn't care anymore. I slipped deeper into the depression that I'd been battling most of my adult life. Mostly though, I just lay in bed, sinking deeper and deeper into the mattress as I gained pound after pound. The things I wanted most in life—a wife, children, to love and be loved—had never been further from reach. I barely made it to my two part-time jobs. I barely made ends meet financially because I was spending so much money on food and didn't actively seek full-time employment. I was tired of worrying. I just didn't care anymore.

As bad as things were emotionally, they were even worse physically.

Driving my 1988 Silver Dodge Caravan was one of the last vestiges I had of a normal life. To be truthful, I was a hazard on the road. There is danger—and irony—with jamming 700-plus pounds into a minivan. The steering wheel dug into my stomach, making turning difficult. The seat was pushed all the way back and reinforced with a tire wedged between it and the middle seat. The seat belt wasn't even an option and to operate the window handle, I had to open the door. My thigh was scrunched tight against it otherwise. Giving up driving would have shut the door on any semblance of independence, and I was willing to put myself and others at risk.

When I arrived at CCAC to teach my night course in introductory sociology, I parked in a handicapped space so I could be as close to the building as possible. Even so, I faced an ever-increasing struggle to walk to my classroom, stopping several times to sit, gasp for air, and wipe the sweat from my brow. Whenever possible, I'd hold the class outside near a parking area or in an inside study area closer to my car. Other times, I called off or had others fill in for me.

On the weekends, I worked as a deejay at a local bar and it, too, was proving difficult. Sitting for four hours straight was very uncomfortable. I was too embarrassed to leave the back corner where my equipment hid me from the patrons. Sometimes it meant fighting the urge to use the restroom until I got home. My size made using the facility there nearly impossible anyhow. When leaving for the night, I'd wait for the bar to empty before slipping out into the alley through the kitchen door, which provided the closest parking space and afforded a lesser chance for people to see me and laugh.

Anytime I left home, I orchestrated my every movement. My mind was consumed with finding the closest parking space and easiest entrance. Wherever I went, I carried my own metal-framed chair to ensure I had a place to sit. I had to. Society is just not set up to accommodate obese people. Whether it's a doctor's office, a movie theater, or a restaurant, chairs are often too flimsy, have arms that make sitting impossible, or are too close to tables to use.

I hadn't been inside a supermarket, mall, restaurant, or bank for a few years, opting to use home delivery and drive-through windows. Going out in public meant physical agony, as well as enduring the stares, nudges, giggles, and disgusted expressions on people's faces. Sometimes, out of frustration, I would say something back or look at them in a way to make them uncomfortable. As much as I was used to it happening, it still hurt. I was so appreciative that Terry Bobick, the wife of a support group friend, Randy Bobick, did most of my shopping for me.

With each passing day, my world became increasingly confined to my bedroom, where my computer, telephone, fax machine, and television provided me with ways to live what was left of my life without exerting much effort. The edge of the bed where I sat had a permanent indentation from my weight. I'd get winded taking the few short steps from my bed to the computer. Although I was forty-one years old, I had to rely on my mother for my everyday needs.

Hygiene was a big problem. My crotch and the back of my knees were galled, a bloody irritation caused by lack of air to the skin, and they smelled because I could not reach to clean them properly. Despite my large intake of food and drink, my trips to the bathroom became fewer. Sometimes I'd fight the urge to go for more than an hour because of the pain and effort required to get up on my feet, even though I was using buckets beside the bed to relieve myself. Truthfully, I could not direct the flow of urine into the toilet because I couldn't reach my genitals. Sometimes I ended up with it on me. At my worst, I would allow the bucket to fill up, then dump it out my bedroom window, which required less movement than walking to the bathroom. Nor could I reach my private areas to wipe myself after defecating. Only after my brother David installed a flexible showerhead was I able to clean myself, though not always thoroughly. Getting in and out of the shower was like an Olympic event because of my size and limited mobility. I got hurt a few times, cutting my legs on the sliding door tracks, and it scared me. Sometimes rather than struggle, I'd go dirty for days.

Other people noticed the odor I'd learned to ignore. Some were brave enough to mention it to my family members. In a few extremely awkward and embarrassing moments, David came right out and told me that I smelled. But dealing with it was not something I could handle physically.

The years of carrying excess weight worsened the degenerative arthritis in my knees. I had what I called "Motrin days" when the pain was so intense that I could not leave my bed. The tops of my feet were grotesquely swollen into fluid-filled pillows because my circulatory system was unable to operate efficiently. I had recurring bouts of cellulitis, a potentially life-threatening infection that caused my legs to turn red and fill with fluid. I also bruised easily.

Spiritually, I was at a low point, too. My spiritual growth as a Christian blossomed in the early 1990s after I had lost 330 pounds and was down to my regular weight. But as I became complacent in my recovery, the arms of my addiction slowly embraced me again, and I started to stray from the fellowship of the church and from God. By Election Day 2000, when the rest of the world was absorbed in the Bush-Gore battle for the presidency, I was waging my own inner war. In the early morning hours, while the television talked Electoral College votes and recounts, I wrote to my good friend Patti Tomashewski: "Now, as I try with all my might to fight my condition, I am continually defeated. In short, I'm in bad shape and God's the only one who can help—so I must turn to Him—daily."

At the time, I was reading Neale Donald Walsch's *Conversations with God, Book 2: An Uncommon Dialogue.* One passage in particular struck a chord with me: "You might start anew by realizing the truth of your walk, seeing yourself as you really are."

After months of inner turmoil, my turning point had finally come. I told Patti that I was starting to grow closer to God again, that I was beginning to feel less afraid, and that I had begun to feel some willingness to fight back. I also told her that I had started researching the possibility of stomach surgery to help with the physical recovery that my body so desperately craved.

My physician, Dr. Robert Crossey, had suggested such a procedure to me before, but I would have nothing to do with it. I simply wasn't ready for something that drastic. Dr. Crossey always treated me with respect, so I went to see him as the first step when I began contemplating the surgery. He told me the risk of the surgery was far less than living with my condition.

Calling Dr. Crossey was in part a result of the meeting I had with my older brother, Lee. During our conversation, Lee handed me a simple green-and-white brochure from a Dr. Weaver about an operation called vertical-banded gastroplasty. It was one of several bariatric surgeries more generically known as "stomach stapling." The brochure landed in my hands in a roundabout way. John Robl, an acquaintance, had given it to my friend, Tim "Luke" Wyland, who then approached my younger brother, David. John felt it would be better for a family member to present the idea to me rather than someone who I did not know as well. John is a friendly man who had undergone the surgery and was experiencing success. He hoped that perhaps it might help me, too. David then gave it to Lee.

On January 23, 2001, I had my first appointment with Dr. Miles Lance Weaver, then a general surgeon at Allegheny General Hospital on Pittsburgh's North Side. John told me that Dr. Weaver was a great guy, and no matter whom I asked, including former patients I met on the Internet, I received only glowing reports about him.

I was somewhat embarrassed that I had to get weighed on a special scale sturdy enough to accommodate people up to 1,000 pounds. It had been years since I had been weighed and I really had no idea how many pounds I carried. When I saw the red numbers light up on the scale, I was dazed—746 pounds! I had no idea my weight had climbed so high.

Dr. Weaver told me immediately that he could help me, but he was also very blunt with me. In my state, he told me, I would be lucky to make it to age fifty. I was already forty-one.

Deep inside, I knew that I could drop dead at any moment. The clock began ticking that day. Very loudly.

10

"CUT ME, MICK"

G od had put two choices on my plate. I could continue to commit a slow suicide with a knife and fork, or I could undergo surgery to radically alter my stomach and make a commitment to forever change the way I eat.

Vertical-banded gastroplasty (VBG), or any of the other bariatric surgeries, are usually performed only on those who are really heavy— 100 pounds or more overweight—and only after conventional weight loss options have failed. In 1990, I spent fifty-two days at St. Francis Hospital being treated for food addiction and depression. With the help of the program there, I was able to lose 342 pounds, dropping from 557 to 215, using a conventional diet, an exercise program, and support groups. I started to relapse by treating recovery as an event. I wanted recovery to be over and to get on with my life. I went back to college and slowly dropped all the things that helped me get healthy. Over the next decade, I not only regained the 342 pounds I lost, but added another 200 pounds.

Ed at his heaviest weight – 746 pounds – a week
before the surgery. (Courtesy Gateway Associated
Photographers)

Before I gave in to defeat, I needed to learn as much as possible
about the VBG surgery. The surgical procedure creates a small one-
ounce pouch in the upper stomach. A Gortex band is placed at the
pouch's outlet, limiting the amount of food the body can take in. This
tool would help me feel full for prolonged periods by slowing the
movement of food from the pouch, like water empties from a sink. I
had some concern because, eventually, the pouch stretches to a
capacity of three or four ounces, but it is still much less than the one-
and-a-half quarts held by a normal stomach. What I liked most about
the VBG, as compared with other stomach surgeries, is that it didn't
rearrange or bypass the intestines, and, aside from altering the stomach,
it allowed for a normal flow of food.

My biggest concern was the amount of anesthesia needed for

someone my size. Heavier people require greater doses than the general population and, at 746 pounds, this really frightened me. Additionally, although my cholesterol and blood pressure were generally good considering my weight, I did have problems with sleep apnea. I was fortunate not to have the many other life-threatening problems associated with obesity such as diabetes, heart disease, gallbladder disease, and cancer. Dr. Crossey's words, that living morbidly obese was more a risk than the surgery, began to make sense.

I was—and am—too much of a fighter to throw in the towel. And I could not throw away the precious life God gave me, no matter how many trials I had been put through. I felt like Sylvester Stallone's character in one of my favorite movies, *Rocky*. During the fight against champion Apollo Creed, Rocky's eyes were so swollen from taking Creed's punches that he could no longer see. Rocky was no quitter. "Cut me, Mick," he told his trainer, who proceeded to slice his eyelids with a razor blade to release the fluid build-up. I had taken too many punches from two decades of food addiction. The real me, the athlete buried under hundreds of pounds of fat, and two decades of food addiction, was ready to fight again.

"Cut me, doc."

Well, it wasn't quite that simple.

First, there was no way I could pay the cost of the surgery, estimated at $40,000 (in 2001 dollars), out of pocket. I had no health insurance through my employer since I was only a part-time faculty member. I had no choice but to apply for government-sponsored Medical Assistance. I was so physically compromised that I couldn't make it to the downtown Pittsburgh office to apply. Fortunately, the staff there permitted me to send Lee as my representative. Pleading with my caseworker, who had assigned me to another plan, Lee finally convinced her to enroll me in the health insurance plan accepted by Dr. Weaver.

Second, I had to complete a psychological exam and attend a required pre-op class given by Dr. Weaver's assistant, Linda Eyman, a registered nurse. On the day of the class, Lee dropped me at the door with my metal-framed chair in hand. I would walk several feet, then have to put the chair down and sit so I could catch my breath. Strangers stopped to ask if I was all right, and, even though I was extremely bothered by the unwanted attention, I politely answered, "yes."

Eventually, I made it to the classroom. Looking around, although everyone in the room was overweight, I was definitely the one in the worst shape. When it came time for lunch, I didn't leave the room. I was already in pain from sitting so long and walking would have only added to the discomfort. One of the women in the class was kind enough to bring me back a diet soda. I understood that people had to eat because of the length of the class, but eating in the middle of learning how we were going to alter our insides because we couldn't control our food intake seemed strange, like an Alcoholics Anonymous meeting at a bar. By afternoon, I was even more uncomfortable from sitting for such a long time and, as much as I wanted to listen, I found myself hoping it would soon be over.

The class was informative and it made one point very clear—that surgery was only a tool. To make the tool work, I would have to follow the prescribed food plan—two twenty-five-minute periods of consumption a day and only non-caloric liquids. Having a third meal or eating for too long could mean either stretching the one-ounce pouch created by the surgery or adding calories that would slow weight loss.

I struggled through several weeks, anxiously waiting for word that the medical insurance would pay for the procedure. The call finally came, and my surgery date was set for March 7, 2001, only a little more than three months after I had made my decision in favor of the VBG. From the day Lee first approached me with the VBG brochure, I had strong feelings that God was carrying me through this. Things fell into place too easily for me to write it off as luck. He was answering my prayers.

A few weeks before surgery, I decided that I wanted to help others who were suffering because of their weight. I thought one way was to offer the local weekly newspaper a chance to follow me through my surgery and recovery. I contacted Terry Tierno Stitt, a family friend and columnist for the *Penn Hills Progress*, who put me in touch with an editor.

Six days before surgery, I met with a feature writer, Zandy Dudiak, who would follow my progress for several of the weekly newspapers in the Gateway Newspapers chain. I told my mom, who was skeptical and opposed to me having surgery anyway, that Zandy was a teacher with whom I worked. Mom made herself scarce when Zandy arrived, so I didn't have to explain the photographer who accompanied her.

It was both embarrassing and a relief to finally share the details of my condition with someone. I felt comfortable with Zandy right away. This initial interview enabled her to see me at my worst, giving her a baseline to begin recording my recovery. Both she and the photographer left with a clear picture of the "before."

Putting myself out there in a newspaper was one thing, but I was quite shocked two days before surgery to receive a call from the hospital asking me if I'd be willing to be interviewed on television about my impending surgery. Marilyn Brooks, health editor for WTAE-TV in Pittsburgh, had contacted Dr. Weaver's office about doing a story on VBG and asked for the name of someone about to go through the surgery. Within hours, all 746 pounds of me was broadcast in living color to thousands of viewers in the Pittsburgh area. I felt like I was being smacked each time Ms. Brooks repeated my weight.

I was pleased to receive encouraging calls from many friends who saw the segment, yet I was both surprised and mortified at seeing myself on the television screen. I had been avoiding cameras and mirrors for years. In my mind, I just didn't see myself as being that heavy, even though I knew deep down that's how others saw me. I was disgusted and though I never told anyone, part of me regretted doing the TV spot.

———

Surgery day finally arrived. I was met at the door by caring staff with a rolling bed large enough to accommodate me and save me from having to walk any further.

Except for the medical personnel coming in and out, I was alone in a pre-op room in the Ambulatory Care Center on the eleventh floor of

Allegheny General Hospital in Pittsburgh. No family members or friends were able to be with me that day. That bothered me and added to my nervousness, but I knew there comes a time in the process when I must step away from loved ones, trust the doctor, and be with God.

So, I tried to focus on other things. I had the best room on the floor, a multi-window view of downtown Pittsburgh and PNC Park, the new stadium then under construction for the Pittsburgh Pirates. Three Rivers Stadium, where I had once hoped to play ball, had been imploded to make way for Heinz Field, the new Pittsburgh Steelers stadium. My dreams of playing there had imploded, too. PNC Park held hope for a new beginning for baseball in Pittsburgh. The Pittsburgh Pirates and I both were looking for new beginnings.

The nurse put me through the standard routine, checking my blood pressure, taking my temperature, having me sign papers, and discussing whether or not I had a living will. She noticed that I had ESPN on the tube and was kind enough to take some time to discuss baseball with me, helping to distract me if but for a moment.

As she was leaving, Zandy arrived to do our agreed-upon, pre-op interview. Even though I had just met her the week before, I was relieved to have someone I knew to talk to because I was getting really nervous. I told her about my worries, that even though I knew the surgery had helped others achieve their weight-loss goals, I still had to face the challenges of being a food addict after the surgery. Surgery could not remove the addiction.

I was also concerned about how I was going to get home with an eight-inch incision in my stomach. I could hardly move and adding the trauma of surgery worried me. Getting to the hospital that morning had been a feat in itself.

My brother David had driven me to the hospital in his van. I hadn't been in anyone's vehicle but my own for so long, the only way I could conceive of getting anywhere was to sit in the back of a van. Fortunately, David was able and willing to help. I had the idea that if I could slide in on a piece of cardboard, it might make the process a little easier. It took fifteen uncomfortable minutes. I couldn't imagine doing that with a slice in my belly.

Harder than that had been saying goodbye to my brother as he dropped me off at the hospital door. I am fortunate to have a family that has always been extremely supportive of me, even though I caused them endless worry as they watched me deteriorate physically. But for all the understood love we have for each other, the Adams family is just not physically demonstrative.

David shook my hand as he said goodbye. The truth is, I required a hug.

I told David that I loved him. What I really wanted to tell him was, "If anything happens to me, tell everyone I love them." I held back my feelings; expressing that much emotion was pushing the Adams' family limits.

———

"Let's rock and roll," I told the nurse when it was time to head to the operating room. Zandy patted my shoulder as she wished me luck and said goodbye. Several staff members came in to help navigate the "big boy bed" and my heavy body down the halls.

By the time I reached the operating room, the sedatives were already starting to kick in. As I became more comfortable and was finally surrendering to my fears and concerns, Dr. Weaver asked the near impossible of me. Because they could not lift me, I had to climb onto step stools and then onto the operating table. The hell of being so heavy was shoved in my face yet again. Somehow, I hoisted myself up and on.

As much as I had prepared for this surgery, I was unprepared for how my life was going to change. Although I was somewhat numbed by the sedatives, I knew one thing for certain—I could not go on living without some kind of radical change.

Any last-minute doubts were fleeting. More than anything on earth, I wanted my life back.

11

MIRACLE OF MIRACLES

The weight poured off. Miraculously, just twenty-two days in, seventy-three pounds had melted off my body. As I watched the digital numbers light up on Dr. Weaver's office scale, tears filled my eyes. It had been so long since I'd been moving in the right direction and my emotions spilled over as I saw a "6" as the first number instead of a "7." The tears weren't so much because of the actual number—673—but that I finally had hope for a happy future.

For the most part, my surgery had gone well. I was a bit disoriented coming out of anesthesia, due in part to the large amount of sedation that had to be given to me because of my size. During the middle of the first night, I couldn't catch my breath. When a nurse asked me where I was, I told her "Turtle Creek," a small town about four miles from my home in Penn Hills. In my drugged state, I thought I had been in a car wreck.

Dr. Weaver arrived at 3 a.m., a can of diet soda in hand, to reassure me that everything was fine. His caring nature, as well as his surgical skills, made me glad I'd chosen him for this life-altering procedure.

Unexpectedly, on the third day post-surgery, I ended up in the intensive care unit. A monitor on my finger detected significant drops in my oxygen levels as I slept. I was diagnosed yet again with sleep apnea, a complication that kept me in the ICU for three days, pushing back my anticipated discharge date. Although the apnea could easily be treated using a CPAP (a face mask that forces oxygen through the nose and mouth), I wanted no parts of it. To me, it was C-CRAP!

Those first few days in the hospital, my diet consisted of clear liquids. By the time I was ready to leave for home, I'd graduated to a full liquid diet. In preparation for my arrival at home, Mom had filled the fridge with yogurts and puddings, and the pantry with Cream of Wheat and soups.

Getting home was a major feat. With the ride to the hospital in David's van still fresh in my mind, the thought of 700 pounds of me with a 10-inch, stapled-shut incision in my belly getting into any vehicle—well, from my perspective, it just wasn't happening. I tried to get an ambulance transport home, but it wasn't covered by insurance and I couldn't afford to pay out of pocket. Dr. Weaver even called Marilyn Brooks of WTAE-TV to see if she could help, but that was a dead end, too.

God was certainly throwing miracles my way that March, this time in the form of my pastor, Doug Rehberg. He came to the rescue just an hour before I was slated for discharge. I rode the ten miles home on the floor of his van. Again, cardboard made the slide-in easier. In addition, the hospital staff had kindly packed several pillows around me for comfort, but the ride was still pretty painful. So was negotiating the thirty-foot sidewalk and the six stairs to my porch. Once inside, I found out the wrong size hospital bed had been sent. Part of being that heavy was making sure I could be comfortable without walking too far or standing too long. I called my hospital caseworker and she got them to send me the same kind of bed I had in the hospital, the one that could sit me up and help me get out of bed without taxing the suture line on my belly. Until it arrived, I had to ease down onto my own bed, and then struggle to get back up. I was in a lot of pain.

Once all was settled and I was in bed for the night, I looked at my belly and wondered what in the hell I'd done to myself. Then I realized I had been on a one-way street to nowhere.

Seeing 673 on Dr. Weaver's scale was like a milepost, a sign that I was headed in the right direction. I purposely hadn't eaten the day of my appointment, hoping Dr. Weaver would say I had sufficiently healed to be able to eat soft solid foods like eggs, macaroni, noodles and mashed potatoes. Those taters were still one of my favorites and I couldn't wait to get home for my first feast—most of an egg, a baked potato, and small glass of skim milk. Later, Mom joined me for my second meal, a half-cup of macaroni and cheese and a small potato. In the midst of all the pain and discomfort, food was still of critical importance to me.

I grabbed for a bucket. I had eaten too quickly, faster than my small pouch of a stomach could handle, and I regurgitated a good amount of it back up. Throwing up after VBG isn't the same as vomiting when you are sick. The motion is gentle, without heaving, but unpleasant and scary nonetheless.

Another time, I swallowed a too-large piece of a pierogie that got stuck in my stomach pouch and wouldn't go down. After a frantic call to the hospital, and the staff assuring me that I'd be okay, I sat for a few hours waiting for the food to move on and the discomfort to go away. My eyes have always been bigger than my stomach, especially now that my stomach was much, much smaller. The addict in me always wants to make sure I don't get shortchanged. This adjustment was going to be a big one. Eating too much now wouldn't make me fat. It would make me sick.

I had no choice but to follow Dr. Weaver's prescribed food plan— two twenty-five-minute meals a day. No more. And to prevent the stomach from sending food back up, I had to learn to take small bites, chew my food thoroughly, put the fork down occasionally, sip liquids slowly, and stop eating when full.

A little at a time, I began to take my life back.

My weight dropped to 648 by two months after surgery, when I finally resumed a normal diet, and to 611 by the end of the third month. My meal choices expanded to include many of my old favorites like pizza, Italian hoagies, Chinese food, and ice cream. The difference was the portions. After four bites of a McDonald's grilled chicken sandwich, I was full.

With my increased mobility, I was able to once again attend services at Hebron Church. Returning to my spiritual base was an important step. I was at a point that I was ready to embrace God as he had embraced me from the day I decided to go ahead with the surgery.

I swallowed my pride, held my breath, and put on a T-shirt and red sweatpants, cut off below the knee, to hide my heavy, misshapen legs. I headed across the street from my home to a fitness center where I could easily step into the indoor pool and swim. Because I could nearly see the facility from my porch, it was hard to come up with excuses not to go. The water made me weightless, so I could give my legs a workout without causing the arthritis in my knees to flare up. I sometimes think I was meant to have gills. I love the water, and this was great exercise to start building back some muscle and burn some calories. Although I felt wonderful in the water, getting in and out was another story. I was uncomfortable when I saw my reflection in the windows as I left the pool. In my mind, especially now with some weight off me, I just didn't envision myself the way I looked.

By the end of May, barely three months after surgery, I was able to return to my adjunct teaching job at the community college. A few weeks into the summer session, I arrived in class with a doughnut shop bag, which I sat in clear view on my desk. The bag drew stares from the students, who had heard my tale of morbid obesity just the week before. I smiled—and so did they—when I pulled out a large cup of black decaf coffee, no cream, no sugar. Teaching was a vital part of my life. It did more than bring in a paycheck. Teaching made me feel useful and not so much like a slug, which is how I sometimes felt in my most self-deprecating moments.

I also got back in the spin at my bar deejaying job. Sitting for long periods, both teaching and deejaying, was markedly easier now than it had been prior to my surgery.

For the first time in two years, as the softball season got into full swing, I was able to navigate the steps down to the ballfield at Universal Park in Penn Hills instead of sitting on a bench on the hill above it. I was able to return to the bench to coach and keep score for Inn the Ruff, my brother David's adult men's team.

I was on a roll.

In early June, I began what I called the "Mr. Ed Reclamation Project." Even though I did not fit into his chair comfortably, I visited the dentist several times for extensive work to improve my appearance and health. I got fitted for new glasses, choosing a frame befitting a college teacher. I began to grow back my mustache, something I had done on and off since high school. I began buying bright-colored clothes instead of hiding in the dark blues and blacks that comprised my size 7X wardrobe. Now, the 6Xs and 5Xs hung loose. I wanted people to see the new me. I was finally able to reach and clip my toenails and put on socks for the first time in two years.

I even started a credit counseling program to work toward eliminating the debt that accumulated during the time when my eating was out of control and the period when I was unable to work. Being an out-of-control addict is expensive.

Everything was going my way—or so it seemed. I was talking the talk.

In early June, Zandy had finished the four-part series documenting my road to recovery for Gateway Newspapers. Because she realized the sensitive nature of putting someone's life out for public scrutiny, she broke company policy and decided to let me read the stories prior to publication. Because I couldn't wait to see my life unfold in words, I began scanning the pages while waiting in the drive-through line at the bank. Reading about my struggle, my life, touched me.

"You made me cry," I told her on the phone as soon as I'd finished.

Zandy had been in contact with a local radio host who was interested in interviewing me to promote the series during a segment on his show. I was all for it. Remember, I'd had 746 pounds of me broadcast in living color on television screens throughout the Pittsburgh area. So why not talk on WEDO-AM about losing 150 pounds?

A day or so before the interview, the deejay, Gary Greisinger, known professionally as Gary G, called Zandy with concerns that I wouldn't be able to negotiate the steep, narrow stairs to the second-floor studio.

"You don't understand. This is Ed Adams," she told him. Later she told me that after watching how I'd jumped back into life, she had no doubts that I would make it up those stairs. That was probably the day our reporter-interviewee relationship began to turn to friendship, too.

The interview went well. And the newspaper series drew a surprising number of responses, many from people who, like me, were trying to claw their way out of the rut of food addiction or fight morbid obesity. I answered several phone calls and enjoyed running into people who had read the story or seen a follow-up segment that Marilyn Brooks did for her Heathy4Life segment on WTAE-TV news. A side benefit was that I didn't have to explain anything to them. They already knew my story.

I was finally ready to put myself to the test. I had avoided stores for a few years, not only because I didn't have the energy and mobility to walk the aisles and stand in check-out lines, but because I didn't like it when people gawked at me. I asked Zandy to accompany me to a local discount drug store to see how people reacted to seeing me. To my disappointment (I wasn't as important to the world as I thought I was), or maybe delight (that I was never stared at and laughed at nearly as much as my mind led me to believe), no one really gave me much more than a second glance, if that. That day, another door opened on my way back to normalcy.

By the end of summer, I had traveled with the softball team to tournaments in Dubois and York, Pa. I even flew with them to a tournament near Atlanta, Ga., booking an extra seat in the plane for myself, both for comfort and so as not to crowd the person next to me. Although the Sept. 11 terrorist attacks took place only nine days before my flight, any apprehension I had about flying was overcome by the delight that I could travel at all.

One day, I was so busy enjoying my life again that I forgot to eat. Then there were days when the addict in me was bending the rules. I hated when my chicken-shaped timer let me know that my twenty-five-minute meal period had ended. As an addict, I owned my mealtimes. Even if I felt full, I was compelled to continue eating if the timer was still ticking. Whatever was on that plate belonged to me. I began stretching the time limits a bit, and sometimes the number of times I ate a day. And I snuck in a snack or two, too.

Nighttime has always been hardest for me. Now, with the weight continuing to drop because of the wonderful tool that my new stomach was, I had renewed hope for those things in my life I longed for. But when you're tired at the end of the day, hope isn't always enough to fill the night. Food helps.

With food, I could not—and cannot—be trusted one inch. On those lonely nights when I sat alone laundry listing what I didn't have in my life, food was there, an old friend that never said no.

My changing relationship with food mirrored that of a human relationship. Sometimes I felt the loss of comfort and security that food brought me. Eating right was almost like breaking up with a girlfriend.

Addicts require attention—at least this one does. I was back in the game of life at work, on the softball field, in the bar. The newspaper and radio coverage put me in the spotlight, like I had been in my ball playing days. People were very supportive of the noticeable changes in me. And I liked it.

I knew I couldn't do this alone. I turned to Dream Weavers, a support group comprised of Dr. Weaver's patients who had undergone or were anticipating having the VBG surgery. No one has a better understanding of what I was going through than someone who has been through it themselves. Some of the Dream Weavers had been in the initial pre-surgery class with me and they became tremendous supports for me, especially in the early months post-surgery. Because of the response to the newspaper stories, I decided to also start my own support group, Diet Busters, to provide the same opportunity for people living in the eastern suburbs of Pittsburgh. With some success of my own under my ever-shrinking belt, I was ready to help others struggling.

As soon as the newspaper series had run, I talked with Zandy about the idea of telling my story to a broader audience. We agreed to write a book about my life from the days when the Major Leagues scouted me to the new life the surgery had given me.

I also took her up on a challenge issued early in my recovery—to walk with her. We started slowly, a slow gait from bench to bench in a cemetery and park, progressing to longer walks within the reach of some bleachers at a local school. With her patience and my persistence, by October 29, 2001, I was able to walk one mile—something not many men over 500 pounds could do, or would even think about doing. The athlete in me was alive again. Even as the weather grew colder that fall, we kept up the routine, switching to Monroeville Mall when winter arrived.

Sometimes, I actually forgot I was heavy.

One of the rewards of recovery was a more normal relationship with my mom, who had selflessly cared for me at my heaviest when I needed assistance with everyday living. During the worst times, she suffered the brunt of my anger over my situation. Now, I was able to resume some household chores and shopping, and encourage her to join me, instead of the other way around.

When Thanksgiving 2001 rolled around, I had so much to give thanks for. Mostly, I was thankful that God had enabled me to return to my life.

Just a few days later, I began feeling a bit sick. I was having a dull, aching pain in my stomach. When the pain didn't subside, I drove myself to the Allegheny General Hospital emergency department, afraid that something had happened to the stomach pouch. Tests revealed that it was my gallbladder. Surgery was scheduled a few weeks before Christmas. Dr. Weaver was unable to perform the surgery laparoscopically because my intestine was in the way, but he did use the same suture line to spare me any more scarring.

It was a minor setback, but happening just before the holiday, it sent me into a bit of depression that worsened the week between Christmas and New Year's Day. The holidays were never a great time for me and I hated the idea of going into the hospital again.

12

TORN BETWEEN TWO WORLDS

L ife is full of ups and downs. As my weight continued to fall, my life was on a steady climb up for the first time in a decade. I called it the post-surgical "honeymoon period," where I was embracing the bliss of my new life instead of continuing my love affair with food.

But around the first anniversary of the surgery, things began to slow down. Instead of the weight dropping off rapidly, it wasn't dropping off at all. I told myself that it was simply a plateau period, but the addict in me knew the truth. I wasn't following the food plan and it was showing in the numbers on the scale. More than anything, I wanted to crack the 300-pound loss mark. But the scale wasn't budging off 451, just five pounds short of the milestone weight.

Still, the freedom I felt being nearly 300 pounds lighter kept my spirits up. I was exercising regularly and getting out more. I bounced back quickly from the small bouts of depression after an occasional attack of cellulitis, an infection caused by poor circulation that caused my legs to swell and turn red. And I overcame the low period following gallbladder surgery in December. Even the loneliness and sadness I felt on New Year's Eve disappeared in a few days.

I can't say exactly when it started or why, but about thirteen months after the surgery I started to fall into a funk.

One event that may have helped kick off the depression was when I tried to donate blood during a drive at the college. The tables where donors were required to lay could only hold people up to 350 pounds. For the first time since my surgery, I was told I couldn't do something because I was too heavy. I didn't react very well. I was angry. I asked them to let me sit in a chair instead but they had to follow regulations. All I wanted to do was give blood!

Ed, at 400-plus pounds, decided to enter the 5K Race for Pace, finishing last, but finishing. (Photo by Zandy Dudiak)

Instead, I drove a few miles to a blood bank office where they were able to accommodate me. It didn't matter. The initial rejection was a throwback to a mindset of things being taken away from me because of my weight.

Another contributing factor may have been writing the chapter for this book on the turning point in my life, breaking up with my high school girlfriend Chris, and losing my baseball scholarship and my chance at pro ball. As I relived the events during the writing process, I realized how different life could have been if I'd only been able to control my eating and get back on the diamond in South Carolina.

I began feeling even more depressed. I knew what I needed to do to fight it—start following the food plan more closely. But when night-time came and I was alone once again, food was my companion. Sure, my mom was in the next room but that's not what I needed.

I had always been a night binger and I was still taking my last meal of the day to bed with me. The symbolism wasn't lost on me either. There was that void—wanting someone to be with me at the end of the day—and I was letting food fill it once again.

More and more I felt caught between two worlds. The struggle now was this, the comfort of the extra food and the comfort of being heavy and the protection it gave me versus wanting the new life and all the good things it brings. I felt a definite pull in both directions. There was more of a pull toward the healthy life, but there were days the pull toward the comfort of food and fat was a little livelier than others.

I associated security with food, so much that leaving food behind was difficult. I began to have doubts whether or not I'd be able to succeed in the long run, not only with my weight goals, but with my life goals. I'm sure that doubt could have been used in a healthy way. But, I'm an overeater, a food addict.

That I know what's right or wrong doesn't really matter. Security for the soul overrides all that stuff.

Addicts, and me specifically, on some level, are looking for a life without the pressures of living. Having the addiction eliminates a lot of those problems, even though it causes others. As my recovery progressed, I realized that I should be dealing with those problems, just like everyone else.

When I was 746 pounds, I struggled to move from my bed to my computer. The furthest thing from my mind was trying to get a full-time job. I was worried about drawing my next breath. As my life became more normal, the excuses vanished.

There were things about my life that made me feel so inferior to my peers. No wife. No kids. No house of my own. No full-time job. No medical benefits. Not even a working car of my own. I'd been borrowing my mother's vehicle since mine broke down about four months before.

People don't expect addicts to meet those goals. The increased responsibilities that come with recovery are part of the reason I began to feel the tug between the world of being heavy and the world of being healthy. I now had to face the "risk" of finding a full-time job. I had to prepare myself for the "risk" of an intimate relationship—and what can and might not happen when you put yourself out there.

I always believed that if I got the job, the house, a wife and kids, my problems would be solved. But Doug Rehberg pointed out to me that some people have all those things and it still doesn't solve their problems. The addict is looking for a struggle-free life. The truth is it doesn't exist.

I saw an episode of Oprah where Dr. Phil said overweight people eat out of need and that, until the need is taken care of, there will be a relapse. He also said that once the need is taken care of, sometimes people continue to overeat out of habit.

I couldn't let the addiction win now, not after all I'd gone through.

By May 2002, I had actually worked up the nerve to ask out a former adult student who worked at the community college where I taught. We'd been emailing back and forth and I decided to take the chance. Because I am shy when it comes to relationships and I have a problem with intimacy, this was a big step. When she said "yes" to a dinner invitation, my mind raced ahead. I was ready to marry her by 5 p.m. that day and live happily ever after. She would rescue me from my loneliness, save me from letting food be my only lover. At nearly 43, I was like a high school kid getting ready for his first date.

It ended up being nothing more than two acquaintances having dinner together. She let me know that she already had a boyfriend. Evidently, she thought she was going to dinner with a friend and I played out the role graciously.

In a few hours' time, my dream bubble had burst and I started falling deeper into the funk, letting food embrace me once again. All the progress I'd made over the last year dissolved into self-pity.

I began to recoil, cutting myself off from friends who could help me. When Zandy called to walk with me, I used the excuse that my legs were sore. Truth is I could have walked if I had wanted to. I began to miss church and started to move away from healthy things, such as justifying purchases of snack foods just because I had coupons for them. My marriage to the food plan was getting to be a rocky relationship. I let my Diet Busters support group dissolve because of my own issues.

I still went to the softball fields as the new season got underway. A part of me was elated that I was not just a spectator this year, but a manager and first-base coach for the Inn the Ruff bar team and out there in the mix. I was able to move around so much better than the previous year, when I was only a few months post-surgery. I didn't feel like I was on display and enjoyed socializing at the games and the bar afterward. I even stepped into the batting box and hit once. I let my mind dream.

But even so, there was a part of me that hurt. Of all the guys on the field, I was the only one who'd played for a Division I college team. I wanted to play ball in the worst way. Physically, I just wasn't able.

The funk hit me hard the day of my forty-third birthday, June 24, 2002. Here I was, another year older and still alone. I pulled myself out of bed to teach my summer morning class. As soon as it was over, I called Zandy, whose newspaper office was just across the street from the college. I asked her if she could meet me at a nearby Chinese restaurant for lunch. By this time, she knew me well enough to tell from my voice that I really needed the company of a friend that day.

When she walked into the restaurant, I must have looked pitiful. I admit, I felt pitiful, too. She reached out and patted my hands, which were on the table, and asked if I was okay. Tears began to well in my eyes but I threw up the emotional wall that I always do when my feelings are ready to pour out, stopping the tears before they rolled. I certainly wasn't going to show my emotions in front of a friend, let alone in public. But I was able to talk with her about what I was going through.

I was surprised when she suggested that we share a plate of fried rice, which is always served in heaping portions. Share? With a food addict? Maybe she viewed me differently than I viewed myself. In the end, there was enough to take home to my mom, too.

I had finally reached out for help, the first step in climbing out of the funk.

Only a week or so later, I was ready to break into tears again. I had noticed a bulge in my belly and decided to have Dr. Weaver check it out. It turned out to be a hernia, but not severe enough to warrant immediate treatment. Still, it meant going under the knife one more time. I sat in traffic on the way home, asking myself again and again what more did I have to do to move on with my life.

There was no doubt that this was the lowest point in my recovery to date. I kept trying to convince myself to stay focused on the good things. I tried to move out beyond myself more.

Zandy suggested we change the location of our weekly walks to a more level place that offered half-mile laps around a high school. She felt I could break through to a two-mile walk there because the terrain where we'd been walking was hilly. Even before the funk, I had warned her to watch for signs of me withdrawing, knowing it was how I handled things not going well. What she didn't tell me at the time was she had suggested the change in walking places as a way to challenge the athlete in me, taking a chance that achieving a new milestone physically might help me turn the corner.

I have to admit, it did help.

On July 8, not long after our walk and just a week after my doctor's appointment, I told Zandy, "Ding, dong. The funk is dead." And while there were still some traces of depression remaining, I now had the strength to begin back on the track to a normal life. Getting out of the funk meant taking positive action, forcing myself to get out and walk, get back on track with my eating, and keeping up my social contacts.

I'd met with Doug, and he had told me to be grateful for the talents I've been blessed with and other things that were going well in my life. As I began putting things back in perspective, I knew he was right.

In August 2002, I got a call from Patty Florentine, director of the Supportive Services Office at Boyce Campus. She offered me a job as a reading specialist to help students with disabilities attending the college. Although it was only twenty-five hours a week, it opened the door for me to having a steady day job, something I hadn't had since the days at Pizza Hut. It was a turning point for me. Along with the night classes I was teaching and my weekend disc jockey gig, I was finally going to be earning a decent living.

By September, I was regularly walking three miles with Zandy. The athlete my father raised was blooming once again, just on a different field. The competitor in me decided it was time to move beyond the lap walking and put myself to the test. Pace School, next to the high school where I'd been doing laps, sponsored a 5k run and walk every October.

I decided to enter. I wondered if I was truly crazy, but I knew in my heart that I had to give it a try.

The course followed the sidewalks along a four-lane road, turned around in a residential side street, then headed back toward the school. Though winded at times, I kept a steady pace and pushed through, even up the steady grade along the last stretch. I finished with a time of 1:16:47. But to be 436 pounds and walking what amounted to a twenty-six-minute mile—so what if I finished last. The Adamses always distinguish themselves in some way!

The prize for me that day was being out with people again, pushing my body to the limit, and just finishing at all. The triumph was knowing that nineteen months earlier, I'd struggled for breath just walking across my bedroom.

13

DYING TO EAT

I'm good at being an addict. In fact, I excel at it. I've spent more years perfecting my addiction than I have my baseball swing. I'm sure that given a baseball bat and a thinner body, I could be batting .300 within a few weeks or months. I'm also sure that given an ample amount of food, I could get right back up to 746 pounds in just a few years.

Part of me doesn't care. The addict is winning right now. Ed Adams, the guy who had high hopes for a normal life and an optimistic attitude that VBG was the cure-all, is losing. The addict cares only about where the next meal or snack is coming from.

I am the addict. I don't care about too much else.

I go through the motions of life, keeping busy with work and softball and shopping and anything else to avoid dealing with the realities before me. I've withdrawn from the wonderful support groups that got me through my first two years post-VBG. I've withdrawn from the exercise that was helping me lose pounds or at least maintain my weight on days where I didn't follow the food plan. I've withdrawn from the friends and family members who have supported me and cared about me since my surgery—and in those dark days before.

More frightening is that I've once again withdrawn from my church—and my God. And I've been dishonest with myself.

I don't give a crap. I know that's the depression talking but it's how I feel. I'm tired of running into the same wall. Although I have spurts of energy, I'm exhausted. I'm physically, mentally, and spiritually drained. I have a thousand answers for a way out but I haven't the energy or willingness to do any of them.

I've missed yet another summer of playing softball. Actually, being able to manage and coach and travel with the team to in-state and out-of-state tournaments has been a blessing since my surgery, but this year I wasn't in the shape to go. I know if I had followed the food plan and exercised more, I could have been on the field this year—perhaps a little on the heavy side and maybe not as fast on my feet as before, but at least out there playing the game.

The only game I'm playing right now is in my head.

Oh, I've reached some of my goals. I have the steady day job at the college and the night classes. I have a nice, reliable van. I am still somewhat mobile. I'm close to being debt-free.

My two biggest goals, my two biggest dreams, still elude me. At forty-six, I'm still living at home with mom. And I still don't have "someone."

I guess when I had the surgery, I figured that by this time I'd have a special woman on my arm, someone to come home to, someone to love, someone to love me. Each bite of food takes me further from my dreams. I do take "someone" to bed with me at night. Her name is Suzy-Q, the Hostess brand. Much as I love "her," she isn't going to hold me or kiss me good night. She might as well be the kiss of death. The part of me that still cares is afraid marriage will never come for me now. For one reason, I'm already hitched.

I'm married to food. It is my God. It embarrasses me and I'm ashamed.

I try to think back to my days at St. Francis and the burden that was lifted when I learned food addiction is "an illness, not a personal weakness."

Yeah, well horse shit to that.

I understand the concept but I don't feel that way. I feel God doesn't need people like me who worship ice cream instead of Him. I know in my head that He loves the weakest of the sinners the most. Right now, I feel so unworthy of his love.

I feel particularly crappy when I realize God has blessed me with a good mind and all the knowledge I need to fix this problem. Yet I still reach for food instead of Him.

My physical condition at 746 pounds was abominable. The mental war is worse. It's a private hell I wouldn't wish on anyone, not even people I don't like.

In some ways, I'm thankful my family hasn't said anything to me. I know they know I'm slipping. I know they're beginning to worry. So are some of my closest friends. As much as I appreciate their concern, a part of me resents them interfering. How dare they try to get between me and my food, even though in my heart I know they want to help me and am touched by their actions.

I sometimes wonder what goes through other people's heads. "Yeah, he had that surgery but he's gaining again." A lot of people ask how I'm doing. Funny, but right now they probably care more than I do.

I see myself backsliding. I don't have the strength to just "Stop it!" as I tell other morbidly obese people who seek my counsel. The timer that made sure I kept to two twenty-five-minute meals a day is collecting dust on the headboard shelf of my bed.

Three years ago, nearly two years post-surgery, I was walking three miles at a time—and felt confident enough to enter the 5K walk. Now, I have trouble moving from one room to another. Instead of parking in the regular lot at school to make myself walk more, I just coast into the handicapped space right outside the entrance. My meals are more frequent and longer. The portions are larger and less healthy. I snack. Heck, I even make love to Suzy-Q at lunch in front of my co-workers.

I long for a savior—someone who will rescue me, who will love me, who will replace my yearning for food with a yearning for her. Yet, I don't reach out to my Savior, who can help me. I don't reach out to anybody, even when they stretch their hands out to me.

What investment do I have in overeating and remaining unhealthy and just out of reach of my life's goals?

Maybe it's because the goals that remain are the hardest to achieve. If I'm honest with myself, a good part of it comes down to fear. I'm afraid I'll fall one more time.

First is the relationship with my mom. She has gained weight and is struggling with her own health issues. She has lived without a partner for thirty-four years. In some ways, I fill that void for her. What will she do if I leave her and move into a place of my own?

Beyond Mom is the biggest fear of all, being intimate with a woman. I feel that I've been out of the game for so long, I don't know how to jump back in. And there is this deep-seated fear that if I give my heart, she will leave me, just like Dad left me and Chris left me and Jackie left me and my scholarship—my ticket to the big leagues— left me. It's hard to trust life when life does that to you time and time again. I've been conditioned by life's experiences not to trust that my most cherished dreams can ever come true. So, I am afraid.

It's not the idea of dating. It's not that my body isn't in the best of shape. Heck, I dated someone for a few months last year. But when she wanted to become physical, I backed away. I know intimacy is a problem. But it's also that every time I love someone, they leave me. I still hurt, like Elsa the lion cub.

Maybe that's why it's so hard for me to leave Mom. I don't want her to feel the way I have over and over again.

I feel like I've missed out. Most guys my age have families. Or at least they've had girlfriends. My last really steady girlfriend was Chris and that was three decades ago.

I'm not even sure anti-depressants the doctor prescribed are doing anything. Yet, I don't know if I wouldn't be worse without them. My legs are swelling and I'm having problems with hygiene because of my increased size. I'm scared because I'm over 600 pounds again.

I wanted to end this book with a happily ever after. If I embrace my imperfect life, I can see so many rays of light—the love of family and friends, helping students at work, keeping softball as an active part of my life, the cozy home I've created for myself.

And, it's those things that keep me going day to day.

I will be an addict every day of my life. This isn't the life I would have chosen for myself, but it's the life I have. Maybe there is some purpose here that God has yet to unveil—a reason why He's let me live this long this way.

14

KNOCKIN' ON HEAVEN'S DOOR

I t was supposed to be a simple operation. Well, at least it started that way. I'd had two abdominal surgeries—the VBG in March 2001 and my gall bladder removed about ten months later. My stomach walls were weak and, less than two years out, I developed a hernia on the left side. I'd also had a fatty tumor removed from my thigh in the interim. I'd been in relapse for quite some time, AGAIN! My depression was as bad as ever on top of that. Though I had moments of clarity, most of the time, I just didn't care.

I'm not much for resolutions, but at the beginning of 2006, I decided to begin seeing Dr. Crossey monthly. He increased the dosage of my anti-depressants. I surprised myself by not missing appointments with him and, though I did not stop overeating or going to the bar, the act of keeping the appointments gave me some small satisfaction that I was taking care of myself.

While I was on this small roll, I made an appointment to see Dr. Weaver in April. He wanted to go back in to see if I had interrupted the staple line in the VBG. Over the last several months, I'd begun to explore buying health insurance again. But it was just not affordable. Despite not having insurance, I saw a possibility to get the hernia fixed through a grant from the same medical foundation that paid for the removal of the fatty tumor from my thigh a few years before. The balance of the cost would be only a few thousand dollars out of pocket.

The hernia wasn't painful, so I really didn't need the operation to fix it. But I was hinging my hope for yet-another chance at recovery on Doc Weaver's promise that he would tighten up the VBG while he was in there. I thought if I could only have that done, it might start a spurt of healthy weight loss. I wanted that more than the hernia repair.

After some red tape and a deal with my credit union for a small loan against my shares, the operation was set for Wednesday, May 17, 2006. Dr. Weaver projected a four-day stay and a few weeks of recovery at home. The timing would let me finish the semester at school and maybe even recover in time to teach a class during the second summer session.

The Penn Hills Sports Hall of Fame inducted me in April 2006. Much as I was very proud that my high school talents were still remembered—a recognition that I felt was long overdue—I was uncomfortable being seated before the crowd and having to get up, accept my award, and give a short speech of thanks and remembrances.

A few times, Zandy asked me why I was doing this—risking another surgery. Later, she told me that she didn't have a good feeling about it. While she was sitting at the Hall of Fame banquet, she thought to herself that it was good I was being honored then in case something happened to me during surgery.

Sometimes, God sends us messages that we don't understand until later. Or maybe we just don't listen. It seemed that God did not want me at Allegheny General Hospital that day. Mom didn't want to go to the hospital this time, so Zandy volunteered to keep me company in those moments before surgery.

"Let's bring the camera to take a picture for the book," I told her.

As we took off about 4 a.m., Zandy realized she'd forgotten the pillow she needed to drive my van back home since my seat is stationary and she was too short to reach the pedals. I stopped on the parking pad outside my house and, in the process of getting out, she unknowingly knocked my camera out of the car onto the road. When she got back in, I didn't see it. After moving the car, we'd discovered it had fallen onto the street. We retrieved it and were on our way.

At the hospital parking garage, the automatic ticket dispenser wasn't working, so the bar that lifts to allow the cars to enter would not rise. We had to call security to let us in. Once in the pre-op waiting room, the head of the bed would not raise either, making sitting a bit uncomfortable for me. After registering and doing all the paperwork, I waited patiently for my ride to the pre-op area. The nurse had to call several times because they never showed. We joked that with the camera, the parking garage, and the delay, that there seemed to be a string of bad things that morning that we hoped would not continue with the operation.

Then came word that the extra-large bed they'd ordered for me hadn't arrived. For transport to the operating room, they brought a regular-sized stretcher, cramming in my arms and legs as they lifted the rails.

Before they wheeled me away, I grabbed Zandy's hand for a moment, both with gratitude for her coming along and out of fear of what lay ahead.

The operation went well. Zandy and Doug visited me the next day and, aside from being doped up on morphine, I was recovering nicely and it looked like the four-day-stay projection would be accurate. Later that night, some forty hours after the surgery, I began to have problems breathing. Concerned, I told the nurses and they called the doctor, who put me on oxygen.

The next day, after Zandy had tried unsuccessfully to reach me by phone, she stopped in while on her way back from a newspaper assignment. When she got there, she questioned a nurse about the possibility of blood clots, but he told her breathing problems sometimes happened to heavy people and especially those with apnea. She grew more concerned when I vomited some brown liquid and I kept drifting in and out. The strap on the oxygen mask broke and when it slipped off my face, my oxygen levels dropped rapidly. Not knowing what else to do, Zandy held it on my face until a nurse arrived to fix it. I begged Zandy to stay a little longer and she did out of concern.

Since she was headed out of town for the next few days, Zandy stopped to visit Mom afterward and, without alarming her, told her that a family member needed to get to the hospital the next day. Her journalistic instinct also told her to program the hospital information number into her cell phone because she was concerned I might end up in ICU while she was away.

She was right.

"We need a central line," I heard someone say. Around me, in a world that seemed to be slipping away, a nurse struggled to insert a catheter into my vein as other medical personnel swirled around me. In that bit of consciousness I had left, I figured this was "it." I didn't care anymore if I lived or died. I didn't care if they saved me.

"Don't bother," I told them.

I'd suffered a pulmonary embolism. A clot traveled from my leg, through my heart, and into my lungs, causing the breathing problems. My history of cellulitis and poor circulation in my legs finally caught up with me. Dr. Weaver told my brother that I was "a time bomb waiting to explode."

I was heavily sedated, and put on blood thinners and a respirator. I really have no recollection of the first two weeks in ICU and have relied on my family to fill in the details. Two days after I was put in ICU, the doctors began to talk to them about the "what ifs." Little did I know then about how much my family went through—their prayers and tears—scared that this time they'd finally lose me. Nor did I know about the large number of people from church, work, softball, and my other friends who were praying up a storm for my recovery. Though I hadn't heeded God's messages about the surgery, thankfully He began listening to their prayers.

About five days later, a week after my surgery, I was responding to people by nodding my head. I'd even asked my sister Jody for a notepad and paper, but I nodded off before I got the chance to use it. The doctors hoped to start removing me from the respirator within a few days but warned my family it could take a while. That turned out to be an understatement.

The next day, they removed the respirator and put me on oxygen. But two days later, I was back on the respirator after suffering a setback. I'd developed sepsis, more commonly known as blood poisoning, and had to be given blood. I had some problems with my blood pressure being stable. After scoping me, doctors discovered vegetation (clumps of bacteria and cells) on my heart and gave me an antibiotic to fight it. I also had a horrible bout of diarrhea caused by C-diff, a bacterial infection common in ICUs. The doctors decided to put an umbrella-type filter in my aorta to catch large clots before they reached my brain and lungs, but it had to wait until I was stable enough to withstand another operation. At this point, I was pretty fragile—and out of it.

About sixteen days after my surgery, I began the slow turn around. My first memory of coming to was of being uncomfortable. Tubes down my throat, up my nose, and everywhere else. No eating or drinking. I was being tube fed. I did not have all my faculties yet. I would have moments of being awake and had to use a pad and pen to communicate. My brothers David and Lee visited and later told me I asked via notepad for two diet colas, then one, then water, then ice chips. I wasn't allowed anything. I had no idea what had happened to me, I just knew it was bad.

The next day, Zandy visited me for the first time after getting Dr. Weaver's permission. The nurses started trying to wean me off the respirator. I did only forty minutes, which wasn't good, but it was a start. A few times, I ripped out the respirator and eventually the nurses put me in restraints. The only pleasures in my day were getting my head rubbed with a wet towel and watching television. Sometimes, I still had trouble with people reading my scrawling handwriting or reading my lips. I just wasn't all there. I told Zandy I might be in a different room or lab next time she visited, not grasping that I had a long road ahead before even being able to leave ICU.

Three weeks in, the doctors decided to remove the breathing tubes and give me a tracheotomy, which can hasten the weaning process from the ventilator. Zandy came down the evening of my surgery and was pleased to see me wisecracking by once again calling the CPAP machine a C-CRAP. Then, out of the blue, some ICU psychosis began kicking in. I'd been having nightmares that I was being held against my will and that I was trying to escape. I think the combination of anesthesia and all the drugs I was getting contributed to these nightmares. I told Zandy there were three things that happened to me in ICU, including being naked in a ditch in an alley under a bridge. I begged her to wheel me out of there but she refused.

My room got posted for C-diff restrictions, and visitors had to put on gowns and gloves to prevent them picking up the infection. I don't know what I would have done without the visits from my family, a few friends, and Zandy, who had become somewhat of my personal assistant, helping me with business that needed to be conducted, such as banking and phone calls. A talking trach made communication much easier and I had Zandy bring down my computer so I could feel connected with the world outside.

On June 16, for the first time in the month since I'd come to AGH, I got out of a bed and into a chair for three hours. More importantly, I breathed on my own for four hours. The little miracles we take for granted mean so much when you're knocked down. And when I finally could have fluids, well, I never knew a sugar-free Popsicle could taste so good.

I sometimes struggled with fluids in the trach tubes, but it was so much better than the breathing machine. On June 21, I stood on my own. On my forty-seventh birthday, June 24, Mom, Zandy and I celebrated as I ate a 7-Up ice pop Zandy made just for me at my request. But I was starting to get depressed. I was having very vivid dreams. Sometimes I wondered if I'd ever leave Room 12 in the trauma ICU.

If there was anything good about being in ICU, it was that my friendship with Zandy grew closer. I started having feelings for her that went beyond friendship. It would be a long time before we'd ever discuss it with each other, but I know that I liked feeling this way and that it definitely made me want to do my best to get well again.

At St. Francis, in my first real attempt at recovery from food addiction, I had fifty-two days in lockup. On July 7, fifteen years later, I had reached fifty-two days in recovery from a clot that almost cost me my life. But I was back in a normal room and able to think that I might actually get home again. I was starting back on a soft solid diet. No more feeding tubes. My weight had dropped to 586 since the surgery. What a way to lose weight!

15

I CAN'T FIGHT THIS FEELING ANY MORE

I finally got sprung. As I traveled home along the Parkway toward home with Doug Rehberg in the driver's seat, it was great to breathe in fresh air, especially after having been on a ventilator. I didn't even mind the traffic.

After nearly two months in what felt like solitary confinement in the ICU, struggling just to stay alive, I could hardly believe this day had come. My mind couldn't wrap around the fact that I'd had surgery on May 17, 2006 and it was already July 21.

I'd asked Zandy to meet us at my house in case Mom needed help. It wasn't until I stepped from the car and tried to make it up the few short steps that I realized I was in trouble. Big trouble.

Although I'd had physical therapy in the hospital, being mostly bedridden for sixty-six days had taken its toll on my muscles. It wasn't just the atrophy; it was being too weak to move 586 pounds from the car to the house. Somehow, with Doug's and Zandy's help, and maybe with a little boost of adrenaline, I made it to my bedroom.

My dog Sammy was a welcome sight. And Mom—this woman was nothing short of a miracle in my life. As Doug left, I began to panic. I felt the urge to use the bathroom. How was I going to navigate the short trip across the hallway? I even had doubts that I could lift myself from the bed.

Mom had her limits, too. My mind began racing. Though embarrassed, I had to ask Zandy to go to the nearest pharmacy and purchase a urinal and bedpan—and try to make it quick.

I had immediate regrets about not listening to the doctor and hospital staff when they recommended that I go to a rehabilitation facility for a few weeks to build my strength before tackling the challenges of home. After being at death's door, my only thought was to escape. No doubt, my first weeks at home were among the most challenging of my life.

Mom handled a lot as I recovered. I'll never be able to thank her enough for that. I had visiting nurses, physical and occupational therapists, and worked hard to regain my strength after my hospitalization. I appreciated the support of my siblings through this entire disaster. Zandy was truly my angel as she tried to fill the gaps for us.

The financial challenges were as daunting as the physical ones. I was a little more than fearful about the more than $100,000 in medical bills facing me after my long stay. Joey DiGuglielmo, a talented pianist who was Zandy's work friend, offered to perform a benefit concert to raise money to help with my expenses. They arranged to have it at my church that fall. It was one of the first times I was able to leave the house. I was heartened that so many caring people came out for the cause. Between that, money raised by my Inn the Ruff bar friends, and the hospital's charitable fund, I ended up only have to pay a few thousand dollars out of pocket for the six-figure bill.

My recovery took six months. As always, lack of structure and too much time on my hands are dangerous for me. Triggered by the post-traumatic stress of my hospital stay, I began some bizarre coping skills, not unlike what I'd experienced with eating before my downfall at Carolina.

After Mom and I moved to the new house in 2004, Zandy had given me a pumpkin spice glass jar candle as a housewarming gift to match the pumpkin cream color I'd painted the living room walls. Orange was a comforting reminder of Dad and my childhood days playing for the Astros. I began adding a few more pumpkin candles, and some kind friends helped the cause.

During these months of recovery, I had a credit card, too many hours to kill, and the Internet. I began searching eBay and other sites for unique pumpkin-spice-scented candles. I finally ran out of places on the wall to hang shelves to display them. By that time, I had more than 400 candles to my name. My most expensive one was custom-made for $70. I even named each of the shelves that housed the candles —like the "low-rent district" for the cheaper candles and the "big boy" shelf for the chunky ones. The nine identical Yankee Candles lived on "Murderer's Row," the nickname of the powerhouse batting line up of the 1927 New York Yankees.

The candle obsession was followed by a tea frenzy (and I wasn't really a tea drinker) and a smaller collection of spices. My heart was working on its own obsession, too.

Zandy and I clicked as friends from the beginning. We shared the Penn Hills experience growing up. Though she was four years older than me, we knew many of the same families and teachers. We'd even figured out that we attended many if not all of the same high school basketball games between 1971 and 1973. She jokingly admitted that she was too busy trying to keep her hairbrush and car keys tucked in her knee socks under her bellbottoms to notice a junior high "pip-squeak" like me in the bleachers, even one who would become a star on that court a few years later.

I had to trust her as I shared my story with the local newspaper in 2001 and, in the five years between then and now, as we worked on the book, the bond of friendship between us solidified.

A lot of people didn't understand our friendship, the single man and married woman, but I viewed that as their issue, not ours. They hadn't walked in either of our shoes.

Her husband had been suffering from heart disease and many of its complications since her children were young. In a nutshell, Zandy had emotionally checked out of her marriage by 1998, three years before we met. The entire family suffered as a result of his reactions to his illness. Marital counseling had not helped change the situation.

Zandy stayed in the marriage because she had taken the vow "in sickness and in health" and didn't feel right leaving him or depriving her children of time with their father, in case the worst happened. He continued smoking and not eating healthy foods. His health continued to deteriorate. Occasionally, I put her in the hot seat about her life at home, but it took her a few years to really open up to me about how bad things were.

I truly felt empathy for her husband, knowing how hard it is to deal with chronic illness, but I didn't like what he did to his family. He resented my friendship with his wife, even though he had several female friends of his own, and he made no effort to get to know me or welcome me as a friend of the family.

Though Zandy and I filled a few voids in each other's lives as friends, ours was a strictly platonic relationship.

That all changed for me one day in the ICU. A lightning bolt hit me as I was under the influence of Dilaudid. As I counted the holes in the ceiling tiles out of sheer boredom, I realized I had fallen in love with her. I didn't want to love her that way. I knew it was wrong. I couldn't deny, though, what my heart was feeling. I trusted her more than anyone in the world. I wanted to make her happy, something she deserved. I wanted to treat her like a queen. I had been ready to chuck it all in when I asked the hospital staff to just let me die as they tried to save my life after I suffered the blood clot. Suddenly, I had a reason to get well, better than anything the doctors could have prescribed.

She had no idea about my feelings. I couldn't wait for her visits to the ICU. The time between was torture. Being in love was something I hadn't truly felt since my high school days with Chris. Oh, I was definitely attracted to the wonderful and kind women I'd dated through the years. This was different. As my co-author and friend, Zandy knew all my flaws, my idiosyncrasies, my likes, my dislikes, my issues. I had no doubt she already loved me as a dear friend. She'd shown that to me in many ways in the time we knew each other.

For now, I'd have to keep my feelings to myself. I tried to talk myself out of them but every time I saw her, I knew my heart would win the fight. It was difficult to keep those feelings in check. I prayed a lot—both to be strong morally and recognize when it was the right time to tell her, if ever. The months passed and the years turned. As much as I wanted this, that part of me that was unsure about relationships, and especially about intimacy, held me back from gushing out my true feelings.

Finally, I had to talk to someone about it. I thought Doug, as my spiritual leader, would offer me honest insights. I told him that my feelings had grown beyond good friend status. I confessed to him that I loved her. I wanted badly to tell her how I felt, but she was going through so much at the time that adding more of a burden for her might have been the last straw. I wanted what I wanted—and I was sure—but I was also sure that I didn't want any part of affecting her life in any kind of negative way.

Doug and I spoke of many things. And we prayed.

When her work friend, the late Michelle Brokenbek, was diagnosed with cancer in 2008 and quit work to focus her treatment, Zandy had an awakening. What if she, herself, had a devastating diagnosis and only a few years left? She was a happy person by nature—and she had grown tired of her husband dragging down the mood of the household.

We were at a local Panera Bread, the place where we'd spent many hours working on the book. We were trying to figure how to handle the chapter about my hospitalization. I wasn't ready for what Zandy said next.

"I'm leaving him. I don't know how it's going to go but, if I need a place to stay in a hurry, would you and your mom mind me crashing on the couch for a night?"

I'd been waiting for some sort of sign that it was okay to let the cat out of the bag about everything my heart was holding inside. I looked to the ceiling—looking up at God—closed my eyes for a second, took a deep breath, and let it tumble out.

"I have feelings for you."

That was it. I'd played my hand. She looked surprised for a few seconds and appeared thoughtful. Then she smiled timidly.

"I have feelings for you, too."

And there it was. And there it had to stay. The next move was hers. About a month later, I wrote to her:

My dear,

Though I don't plan on it, if I got hit with a bus today, I would die happy.

I can't thank you enough for caring for me like you do. To be able to love someone and know without a shadow of a doubt on the reciprocation of those feelings, well, you know that has been one of my major stuck-in-the-past issues.

Hope for the future—for "a" future that has some possible definition to it, well, I never had it before. In some ways I'm hesitant to trust it (not you). There are some very real potholes in front of us and I probably won't be off being a little uneasy about that until those things are over.

I can't remember the day (Dilaudid) but it was in room 12—it was a blanket feeling of calmness as I thought of how you were my angel—and that I would like more of that for a long, long time.

The years of being very good friends have set, for my money, an indestructible foundation for us. As cliché as it is, "friends first" does appear to be key.

If it is possible, the past few weeks I have fallen helplessly further in love with you. I can't fathom a life, a day w/o (sic) you. I am smiling as I write . . . for today, I will avoid going near buses and my heart skips a beat at the thought of seeing you again—hopefully soon.

Yours,

e

16

DOWN THE RABBIT HOLE

Here wasn't much doubt before and now there is less that bad times and idle time add up to food problems. It doesn't matter how much I know about all this. That's the way it goes.

You would think the fact that the blood clot almost killed me, that I had to have a tracheotomy, and that I was fed through a tube would be enough. And what about the glorious fact that finally I was in love and that love was reciprocated? Yeah, you already know how this chapter is going to go.

When I was in St. Francis Hospital's Eating Disorders Program, I learned that I was a food addict and that it was a disease. Now, though mental health professionals would likely label me an "eating addict" instead of a food addict, the struggle remains the same.

When Zandy left her husband in 2008, I immediately felt a sense of moral guilt. She was free but I was afraid. I didn't want anyone to think she left her marriage because of me, even though deep down I knew that she planned on leaving before we even discussed our feelings.

Around the same time, my dog Sam, named for the beer Samuel Adams, was diagnosed with lung cancer. I found myself afloat with so many different emotions. Zandy was driving cross country to bring her son home from film school in California when I had Sam put to sleep. I didn't even tell Mom—and she was upset she hadn't said goodbye.

A few days after Zandy returned, without much thought, I got a new puppy, a black lab mix I named Michael, after my middle name.

I've explained before that Mom was not a disciplinarian—and black dogs are my kryptonite. I couldn't train Michael because it broke my heart to be stern. As a result, over the next two years, Michael took over control of the house. He scratched people, soiled the carpet and furniture, and made it unpleasant for the few visitors who made it past the smell. Michael took after me—no discipline, no structure, struggling to be a good boy.

I escaped that reality and thoughts about my physical condition by heading back to the bars in the evenings after work.

Zandy moved to an apartment and her adult children ended up living with their father. Though she understood the moral reasons for me not visiting her there, she was disappointed and lonely.

So, I spent many of my nights alone. She spent many of hers alone. I drank. She wrote a book on local history. I slowly packed on weight again.

In October 2008, I was inducted into the East Boros Sports Hall of Fame, a chapter of the Pennsylvania Sports Hall of Fame. Even though Zandy was there with me, it was a miserable night. Though I was about 100 pounds less than I was for the Penn Hills Sports Hall of Fame, I was very self-conscious.

Being honored brought mixed emotions. There was a part of me that still kicked myself for ever ruining my shot at a professional career, though I was honored that people still remembered the skills I once had.

I needed to go to South Carolina in January 2009 for the National Softball Association Tri-State Hall of Fame. No honors this time, but there was a rules meeting that would help me carry out my duties as NSA Western PA director. I didn't trust my legs enough to make the drive myself, so I asked Zandy to go with me to Myrtle Beach. She didn't hesitate.

That began a series of short weekend trips we took together for my baseball director's duties over the next year, including a return trip to Myrtle Beach the following January.

For my 50th birthday in 2009, she wanted to treat me to something nice. I suggested we head out to Indiana, Pa., where I had attended IUP, and perhaps stay in a place that had a pool. I loved swimming—I think I must have been a fish in my past life! As it turned out the pool was cold, we both seemed to come down with a flu-like illness by dinnertime, and it was the day that Michael Jackson died. The trip was pretty much a bust. But I left knowing that we'd always be there for each other, in sickness, health, cold pools, and deaths of beloved music stars.

After our Myrtle Beach trip, I sometimes stayed at her apartment overnight. Once we got snowed in. Another time, I got very sick and she nursed me back to health. I wanted this all the time. She cooked dinner for me on Friday nights when I'd visit. It was the closest thing to marriage that I'd ever experienced. I still had physical struggles with intimacy, though I'd grown to believe the best intimacy is when you lay down together, laugh, and enjoy each other's company.

Michael was a major problem in moving forward with Zandy. As he'd grown, the problems grew as well. I couldn't admit Mom and I were incapable of handling a rambunctious dog who had no training. I loved him too much to give him up. One of my flaws is hoping a problem just goes away. But it never works.

When her divorce decree was final, instead of moving in with me, Zandy decided to move back into her house because the kids weren't getting along with their father. Her ex-husband moved to an apartment.

Her final decision started me on a slide. I knew that Michael was a factor in her making that choice.

I felt my dreams slipping away.

About four months later, I finally decided that Michael—and Mom —needed a better environment. Zandy volunteered to return him to the shelter where I got him. My heart shattered into a thousand pieces when I patted him on the head the last time. I grieved for a long time. He was like a son to me.

It seemed that I'd finally be able to have everything on my bucket list, except children of my own. But between my nieces, nephews, and Zandy's children, I might be able to enjoy that next generation of babies grow.

A string of health and work issues seemed to knot up those things.

In 2008, a few years after the ICU stint, I suffered a particularly bad case of cellulitis and my kidneys began shutting down from the infection. Fortunately, everything cleared up after some antibiotics and a few days in the hospital.

Then I got shoved back a few more steps. The college cut all my teaching classes because my job as a student support specialist increased to thirty hours. The college's policy stated that teaching an extra class would put me at a forty-hour status and thus eligible for full benefits that would cost the college.

I needed the medical benefits the Supportive Services job provided, even though I had to pay half the cost. I was forced to give up something I absolutely loved doing—teaching. Even worse, losing those classes cut my income in half. Yet another blow in my attempt to get ahead with things.

The rollercoaster didn't end there. I developed a large, open wound on my leg that wouldn't heal. Eventually, I had to have a procedure where the doctor sewed a cow membrane over the wound to help it close.

Maybe some people could have just let all this roll off them. But for me, every blow is a trauma. And the punches kept coming.

It had been a long time since I felt people were staring at me or saying things about my weight the night in 2009 that I pulled up to the drive-through window at a nearby fast-food restaurant. The cashier began talking to his co-workers as he got my food. They all turned and looked toward the window. Then they began pointing and laughing. I wanted to drive away, but I stayed in line and got the food. The experience left me humiliated. I called the corporate office to register my complaint about the customer service. I didn't pull up to that window again for a few years.

My horoscope sign is Cancer and there's no doubt I retreat into my

Cancer-the-Crab shell when things like this happen. The incident smacked my self-esteem down, no doubt. But it was nothing compared to the fallout I'd experience after an incident at a local pizza shop about the same time.

Simply put, I tripped on the way into the shop and fell. I got back up, paid for the pizza, and went home. Over and done, except for a little bruising of my extremities and my ego—until one of the employees, a local guy in his twenties, decided to take the video footage from the security camera and put it up on YouTube under the title *Fat Man Falls into Pizza Shop*.

The video had been posted for more than a year when a friend saw it and mentioned it to me.

I was mortified. My depression dug a hole so deep that it took me more than two weeks for Zandy to pull me out of my shell enough to tell her what was going on. She was infuriated. At her suggestion, I called the owner of the chain, whom she had interviewed for a newspaper story. She knew the pride he took in his business and thought he would likely be upset. The owner had the culprit remove the video. Or so we thought.

About a year later, the video showed up again on YouTube. This time, Zandy called the owner and also let my brother David know. David had been a private investigator, so he used his skills to identify the culprit. This time, with the name of YouTube poster in hand, I told the local pizza chain that I wanted to file harassment charges. This was enough to have the shop manager deal with the former employee. The video came down again shortly afterward, hopefully for good.

Just about a week later, David and his family were dealt a blow that made my problems seem trivial. Their son, Tony, twenty-seven, who was disabled, died unexpectedly in June 2011. While I personally experienced first-hand the death of a parent at an early age, my heart broke to see their family's pain and grief. About this time and in the few years that followed, Lee, Jody, and David also had some personal and health issues that brought me a lot of worry. I felt my world was falling apart around me. It was easier to obsess over their problems than confront my own.

Unfortunately, Zandy still had to keep our relationship somewhat on the downlow because of her ex-husband's control over what money she and the kids received to support the household.

Soon after she moved back into the house, Zandy invited me for dinner. Her ex saw my van and burst through the front door, claiming he needed to borrow a bowl. He made it very clear that he did not want me in "his" home. Then he spent time in the driveway, talking to a friend, who, I learned later, convinced him not to re-enter the house with a baseball bat that he planned to use on me.

I could see the headlines: "1977 WPIAL Baseball Player of the Year assaulted with baseball bat." Though her son changed the lock the next day, the incident made it uncomfortable to visit her home.

The 2012 softball season had just gotten underway when I suddenly developed breathing problems. While I thought the issue might be due to an infection in my leg or possibly a blood clot, it turned out to be sepsis caused by cellulitis. Again, I ended up in the ICU. And again, I almost died.

Zandy told me later that she was worried that this might be "it." She tried to prepare Mom in a gentle way by telling her the severity of the illness but Mom, as usual, didn't worry too much. Zandy also contacted Kyle Jenkins, who had become my right-hand man with the softball league, and let him know I was unavailable for Sunday's games.

After my long hospitalization in 2006, I had set the league up with Kyle and Travis Quarles as assistants so the teams wouldn't suffer as a result of my health. They stepped up to the plate, alleviating that worry for me. And since the semester had ended, any work I had could wait until my return.

When the worst was over, I asked Zandy why she stayed with me. She always smiled and said, "You'll never get rid of me." She never knew how many times I thanked God for that security in my life, especially in sickness.

17

THE COMEBACK KID

S ince my playing days at Carolina, my life has been a yo-yo. Ups and downs. Highs and lows. Usually, at my lowest, something sparked the competitor in me to try again.

That opportunity presented itself when my former high school teammate Tony Lonero came back to Penn Hills on October 10, 2012 to premiere an Italian documentary about his life, "Ride to Finish."

Tony's story and athleticism didn't end when his baseball career did.

In June 2001, as I was recovering from my stomach surgery, Tony experienced debilitating symptoms that were diagnosed as multiple sclerosis. As an athlete, I can attest that there's nothing worse than when your body threatens your athletic spirit. When his mom, JoAnn Bary, sent him a bicycle in 2002, he started riding. The next year, he finished his first grueling Paris-Brest Paris race, the first Italian rider to ever do so.

Though I couldn't wait to see the finished film, I had fleeting thoughts of being ashamed of myself when meeting up with my former classmates and teammates. Before going, I had several kick-myself-in-the-pants moments when my head screamed silently, "Why did you mess it up?" When I arrived for the premiere, Tony looked fit and I looked all of 500-plus pounds.

Some of the opening shots included a few old newspaper clippings of the young, athletic me—carrying the WPIAL championship trophy and with Tony, in our uniforms. One of the interviews was with Bill Deem, Jr., who had been one of my Legion coaches. I was honored by what he said about me and Tony being "phenomenal players" whom he wanted on his team.

I was so proud of Tony's life achievements, particularly how he took multiple sclerosis by the handlebars and rode to his personal victory against the disease.

From our earliest days of playing baseball together, Tony inspired me to do better. Seeing how he responded to his curve ball made me want to try to get back in the game of life. My courage to start over again began to grow. Mustering the energy to start from a point of repeated relapse is downright hard.

I'd already been regularly attending a men's church Bible study, which was starting to change the way I viewed myself and my relationship with Christ. This group gave me the spiritual foundation I'd been lacking for a while.

Mom and I took in an already-trained dog that Zandy knew was about to lose his home. Charlie filled that void in my heart that existed since I gave up Michael. Not only did the little guy cheer up Mom and me, but his energy helped ignite my fighting spirit.

During this time, I also became the chair of the Penn Hills Sports Hall of Fame. Though I'd only served on the Hall of Fame board for a few years, I was honored to lead the group. I relished the opportunity to give back something to the local sports scene.

By early 2013, knowing the success I'd had after my St. Francis weight loss, I decided to try Overeaters Anonymous once again on Saturday mornings to get support from others struggling to embrace a food plan. I made an appointment with Claudia Warner, my therapist from the St. Francis lock-up days, who now had her own private practice. Often, I scheduled my appointment with her following my OA meeting.

Recovery is a lot of work for me. At this point, I was spending about six hours a week getting support to keep my recovery on track.

I decided to try Nutrisystem and started having some success losing weight by sticking to the plan. Mom benefitted with some weight loss, too, because we didn't have bad food in the house. Even when I discontinued the plan, I was able to maintain a semblance of healthy eating.

I made it a point to schedule regular appointments with Dr. Crossey. He put me on a heart monitor in the fall of 2014 and found I had an atrial flutter and an enlarged heart, likely caused or worsened by the apnea. I began a cardiac rehabilitation exercise program to strengthen my heart. Though I rejected the idea of a CPAP to deal with my sleep apnea, I was fitted with an oral device that kept my airway open and allowed me to breathe regularly (until Charlie chewed it up). Sleep apnea can damage the heart valves over time and I was a little more open to the idea of dealing with my nighttime breathing issues now.

I still worked only thirty hours a week, so I set my sights on a full-time job with the college. I interviewed for a position at another campus that was equivalent to my director's job. While I didn't get the job, I felt more confident and hoped that I might slide into Supportive Services Director Patty Florentine's position when she retired in a few years.

Full-time employment and marriage were still on the laundry list that has haunted me all of my adult life. I was so close.

18

THE ARMS OF ADDICTION

O h, 2015 started out great. I'd stuck to the food plan. I was down to my lowest weight since 2010—430 pounds. If I stood just right, I could even see my shoes by just bending my head.

I felt healthier than I had in a while. It was still a struggle to walk down the hall at the college, but it was much easier than it had been in a long time. I was buying smaller sizes and that was a boost to my sometimes-fragile morale.

That spring, one of Zandy's former co-workers, Heidi Dezayas, married her long-time boyfriend Jonathan Winkler at one of Pittsburgh's premier restaurants, with one of the best views of the city. The happy occasion was of the best nights we had together as a couple.

For the first time in ages, I had lost enough weight to put on a suit coat. It felt good and Zandy definitely noticed and complimented me. It wasn't the only first that night. I got onto the dance floor for a slow number with her in my arms. I lasted for the entire song, which was not easy for me. The whole night was romantic for both of us.

Then my sister Jody called. When I told her where we were, Jody asked me if I had popped the question, since the restaurant is a romantic place where many get engaged. Unfortunately, I told her "no" and explained why we were there. But I didn't let that reminder of what was lacking in our relationship affect our evening.

About a year later, when we were discussing it, Zandy told me if I'd asked her to marry me that night, she probably would have said "yes."

"Why didn't you tell me then?"

"I guess because you didn't ask," she replied.

Often, our lives were on opposite sides of the seesaw. As mine was on the upswing that spring, Zandy's started crashing down. Both her adult children developed some serious health problems and her ex-husband's health started sliding, too, creating a burden for her kids that spilled over into our relationship.

The love we shared was rock solid. I never doubted her feelings for me. I'd never loved anyone the way I did her. We were best friends, soulmates, lovers, companions. I was always a one-woman man and she was my angel, my queen, my world. But I was growing desperate to get married. My patience was wearing thin. She had just turned sixty and I was heading to fifty-seven.

In the back of my mind, I always questioned how much time I'd have left, given the array of diagnoses on my chart. Time was of the essence, from my perspective. In the beginning of our time writing this book, I joked with her that in any relationship, I wanted to be married by 5 o'clock. And here it was, several years after the clock struck five and we still weren't together.

At one point, Zandy asked me to talk to my brother Lee, who is a real estate agent, about finding a house that would work for our situation. She even asked me a few times to see the ring size chart I had. I didn't give it to her because I felt she was asking out of pity. She once suggested that we get married but live in our separate houses until we could figure out what to do with her house, my mom, her kids, and all our other baggage.

For me, marriage was not spending my time alone some nights. I needed her there all the time.

There were just some obstacles that neither of us seemed able to surmount.

One evening, while we were returning from a restaurant, Zandy asked me to pull into a parking lot where an old milk delivery truck stood at the entrance to Turner Dairy Farms. Growing up, many Penn Hills families had home-delivered milk from Turner's.

We had a nice talk about how fate brought us together, how right we were for each other, and how we had a future together. So, we exchanged vows there, in front of the milk truck, basically saying the same thing people do when they get married. From that day on, whenever we passed the truck on the way to my house, I'd beep the horn for her, though a few times she beat me to it.

I hit a low weight of 396 pounds by mid-2015. Then I started to backslide a little. To be honest, a lot. Frustration and loneliness always made me turn to the thing that gave me comfort—food. My weight started increasing once again.

Zandy recognized the signs and did everything she could to reassure me that our dreams would work out. It's not that I didn't believe her and deep down I knew that the time she spent with me was often at her own expense in getting enough sleep. But there were nights when her son was so sick that she felt she had to stay home instead of spending time with me. And even the nights we did get together, she was often later than usual or fell asleep as we watched TV. The old tracks started to play in my mind. Dad went away, Chris went away, the scholarship went away, Zandy might, too.

We had plans to go to National Softball Association's national convention, which was being held in Las Vegas in October. I had that all orchestrated in my head. We'd fly out, hit the convention, see some shows, get married. Out there, she couldn't hesitate. No way would she turn me down. She'd forget about the things that were holding her back at home. We'd come back as Mr. and Mrs. Edward Adams. We'd maybe have a church wedding here, then. And a reception. But more importantly, we'd be forced to find a way to merge our households and live happily ever after.

Because of all the time she had to take off work to deal with her children's illnesses, she ended up not having enough vacation days to go to Vegas. I was devastated. She knew I was crushed and I know she placed a heavy guilt trip on herself. I was sliding deeper into the pit that I'd spent the last three years pulling myself out of—and then things got worse.

Mom had been sliding, too, for the last year or so. She hadn't been taking care of herself, was sleeping all the time, wasn't eating regularly. Between my depression worsening and her condition, the house began to slide. With the living room a mess, our world was confined to our bedrooms, the kitchen, and the bathroom.

Because I was struggling with my own life, I wasn't able to give Mom the stability and attention she needed. I began to become a bit passive-aggressive about the situation, hoping that maybe my siblings would step in and help. In October 2015, Jody announced that she was taking Mom to live with her. A part of me was overjoyed, not only for myself, but for Mom. Finally, she'd be getting the care she deserved to have in her eighties. And for me—it removed the burden of worrying about whether I was doing enough for this woman who had sacrificed so much for me during the years.

But at the end of the day, I was lonelier than ever. And loneliness has always been my worst enemy. Always faithful, the arms of addiction were there to embrace me as I went to bed.

Zandy was finally able to take a vacation day, so we set off in early November for Gettysburg, Pa. to attend an Overeaters Anonymous weekend seminar.

While I went to meetings, she worked on the book and toured the town. We had done the same thing in 2014 and had a great time. This time, we found Gettysburg Eddie's, a baseball-themed restaurant dedicated to Baseball Hall of Fame pitcher Eddie Plank, the first Major League southpaw to win 300 games. Food and baseball—couldn't go wrong there!

On Sunday, when it was time to pack, I didn't want to come home. Mom wouldn't be there now. And Zandy wouldn't be there either. Just me and my faithful old dog, Charlie. And food.

The 2015 holidays were rough. Without my job at the college as a distraction during the winter break, I spent the days in bed, sleeping, being morose, daydreaming, kicking myself, digging more of the hole.

I vented a bit about my frustrations with the Zandy/marriage situation to my family at Christmas. I could only hope that 2016 would be a better year.

After I was back at school in January, I focused on the upcoming trip to Myrtle Beach at the end of the month for the annual NSA Tri-State Hall of Fame rules meeting. Zandy was able to accumulate the needed two days of vacation. Still, I was afraid something would come up to wreck our plans. When I picked her up and we drove down the street, I could hardly believe that we'd have four days alone together. It was finally happening.

19

NOTHING COULD BE FINER

A s we crossed the state line from Pennsylvania into West Virginia that cold January day in 2016, I breathed a silent sigh of relief. I felt like a kidnapper who had just eluded capture with my victim in full view. I turned my head toward Zandy, who sat in the passenger seat of my red Kia Sportage, and told her, "We're free. There's no escaping me now."

She laughed. "I guess you're right. You're stuck with me!"

Zandy and I were headed to Myrtle Beach, S.C. for the NSA event. We'd made this trek together in 2009 and 2010, but health and life circumstances had been roadblocks in the years since. I was very apprehensive as we started out, afraid she'd get a call from home and we'd have to turn around. She was a bit nervous because her family had more than their fair share of health problems over the preceding months. As it turned out, the only thing that went wrong on the trip was the speeding ticket I got in Virginia.

We both needed this getaway. The previous year had not been a kind one, to say the least.

We had a wonderful weekend. I went to a softball meeting. She went to the oceanfront to collect seashells. We went out to eat a few times, and saw a comedy show that included a hypnotist. More than that, we talked.

"How about we just stay here in Carolina, Ed," Zandy said, wistfully. "Maybe I can find a job with a newspaper or doing social media for an organization here. Maybe the change would do us good. It's warmer here, too."

I was ready to quit my job and find us a little house by the beach before 5 o'clock.

On Friday, as we were driving down the main highway in the afternoon, we passed a public parking lot near the beach.

"Pull in," Zandy said in such a tone that I immediately obeyed. "You're going to the beach."

"I don't know," I hesitated.

"Yes, you do. I'll get the folding chair out of the back of the car and when you need a rest, you can just plop down until you're ready to go."

When I had started walking after the 2001 surgery, she was the one who challenged me to keep pushing myself. I knew I had no choice now. So, I walked up the wooden walkway. She put the chair down. I walked to a bench at the halfway point. When I'd rested, I walked again. She put the chair down again.

"Only down these steps and we're there," she said.

I navigated the three or four steps to the beach and she set the chair close to the end of the path for me. She sat in the sand.

I hadn't been to the beach in a long time. We sat holding hands, talking, joking, being quiet, listening to the waves. I looked out at the beautiful ocean and thought about my God. He had created this wonder. Each wave, each grain of sand, each bird that took flight, each shell. I was so blessed to make it to the sand, to experience this day.

I thought about the "Footprints in the Sand" poem that so perfectly illustrated how God had taken care of me through my life, even when I had given up. I felt the grains of sand on my feet. I dug them in a little.

On that peaceful beach, I reflected about my time in Carolina playing ball. Had life gone differently, I could have been a Major Leaguer. Had a family, maybe even a grandkid or two. But then, Zandy and I would never have met. I wouldn't have been on this beach with her on a winter day in January 2016. I wouldn't have ever known the deep love that defied the odds and grew out of a friendship that started with writing this book.

And at that moment, on that winter beach in South Carolina, I felt as I had in 1978 on the diamond with the Gamecocks. There was no place on earth I would rather be.

20

THE GOSPEL TRUTH

W hen I met Dick Shorthouse in 1991, I was just beginning to embrace the idea of God as the higher power while working the twelve-step program to help me recover from food addiction. Dick, who also lived in Penn Hills, came to St. Francis Hospital during the time I was in the Eating Disorders Unit. He prayed with me to ask Jesus into my life at a time when I needed a sure foundation for my recovery.

Dick was a regional director for Young Life, a high school ministry throughout the U.S. He and his family belonged to Hebron Presbyterian Church, a large congregation in Penn Hills. I started visiting the church in 1991, soon after Doug Rehberg, who is just a little older than me, had stepped into his role as the church's new senior minister. Though Lee and I hadn't been raised Catholic, as Jody and David were after Dad died, it was the church I was most familiar with because of my family ties. When I heard Doug deliver his sermon, I immediately connected. It was so different than what I was used to hearing during a Mass.

I started to sit about six to eight pews back on the left side of the sanctuary. As Doug talked, I always took copious notes, eager to learn about the Word of God and ask God to apply what I learned to my life.

Doug became more than my pastor. He was a true friend. When he jokingly called me a "compulsive nut," he did it not only because he knew me so well, but also out of love for me as a child of God. I called him "the man behind the pole" because, from where I sat in church, he was hidden from view by one of two large pillars at the front of the church until he took the pulpit.

Within a few years, I was asked to serve as a deacon. A deacon at Hebron was one who sought to meet the real, human needs of those in the church and beyond. Though I was a child in terms of my faith, I felt like an adult in serving Him. I was at my healthiest adult period at the point where I joined the church and I was always grateful that they remained a wonderful part of my support system throughout my ups and downs.

My earthly father had died 20 years before I found Hebron. I realized, as I grew in my faith, that my Heavenly Father would never leave me and I worked to anchor my life in Him. With Jesus as my Savior, deep down I knew that even if I were lonely, I'd never be alone.

Doug and the church members prayed for my health more times than I felt I deserved it. But about the same time of my first stomach surgery, a decade into my church membership, Doug told me he would no longer pray for my weight issues. Given the 746 pounds I was carrying, without saying it, Doug knew that I had some more weighty issues to consider than pounds on the scale.

"I care more about your spiritual life," Doug told me.

Doug lived by the example Christ gave us. When I needed help, whether my legs needed treatments, my house cleaned, or I needed transportation from the hospital, he found someone to help or helped me himself. He was there when I needed someone to talk with about my issues.

Mom was Catholic, but she often accompanied me to church services at Hebron. She felt very welcomed and was happy to be there. When I was doing well, we were there almost every Sunday. When I started to go down the wrong path, I pulled away from the church, even though I knew I needed to be there more when I was faltering.

To be honest, I had a difficult time engaging in a walk with Jesus by myself. While my head and heart embraced the love that God had for me, I found it hard to open myself all the way. Part of that was feeling unworthy of the love the Lord has for me. The good news is that I learned that I was not alone in any of this; everyone has the same struggle and need. That's why Jesus calls His children to walk together.

As I struggled with physical walking during the full-blown relapse in 2011, that walk with Jesus began to become easier when I started attending Men's Grove, an adult Bible study at Hebron. The group averaged about eight to ten men a week. In addition to the Bible, we read books dealing with faith and life's struggles and, most importantly, we prayed together.

The group's leader, Bill Kear, had run the men's softball league before turning it over to me and that familiarity helped me soon feel at home with the others in the group. I'd come to learn that they, in their own ways, were as broken as me. We were all in need of God's grace.

I had a breakthrough moment when I have no doubt the Holy Spirit was at work. I asked the question, "I'm so undeserving, why would the Lord choose me? Why rescue someone like me?" I began to ask other questions and we all prayed together. And I began to open up more about my struggles. Not only that, I began to find myself understanding the true meaning of biblical faith: "The courage to accept being accepted." Theologian Paul Tillich was the first one to set forth the definition, but I found myself growing into it.

Instead of focusing inwardly on my problems as I was prone to do, I began looking at what I had in this life and embracing it with gratitude. I came to appreciate Mom more. Though the future with Zandy wasn't happening as quickly as I'd hoped for, I was thankful for her steadfast love for me. I was lucky for my good relationships with my three siblings.

I might not have kids of my own, but I'd focus on my nieces and nephews: the joy of attending the weddings of my nieces, Elyse Adams to Mike Hacke and Maureen O'Connor to David Funkhouser; the excitement of seeing my youngest nephew Ryan Adams playing basketball for his Catholic school team, and David O'Connor play football for Carnegie Mellon University. I had formed a bond with

Brian Adams during a Florida trip for softball when he was younger and renewed that while he attended Penn State. I was so happy when my niece Rachel Adams stopped in the office to see me while she attended community college. And I was vicariously reliving the excitement of being recruited for a Division I college team when my nephew David Adams was a shining star on Central Catholic's football team.

I'd gotten to know Zandy's daughter, Colleen, when she took one of my classes. I was able to get to know her son, Jonathan, too, and was thrilled to be invited onto the set when he shot an award-winning short film in Pittsburgh in 2013. I was hopeful that we'd become family sometime soon.

Another breakthrough in my spiritual growth came in that same year when the Grove began reading Brennan Manning's *The Raga-muffin Gospel: Good News for the Bedraggled, Beat-Up, and Burnt Out*. It was life changing. Manning was a former Catholic priest who was a recovering alcoholic. His reflections on grace and mercy touched my soul and raised my spirit. Nearly every page had something for me to consume—important timing because I was in my comeback period, losing weight, and becoming more active. Better to feed my spirit than my stomach.

Brennan said so many profound things in *The Ragamuffin Gospel* that spoke to me. He elaborated on what acceptance means:

"To be alive is to be broken. And to be broken is to stand in need of grace. Honesty keeps us in touch with our neediness and the truth that we are saved sinners. There is a beautiful transparency to honest disciples who never wear a false face and do not pretend to be anything but who they are . . . Getting honest with ourselves does not make us unacceptable to God. It does not distance us from God, but draws us to Him—as nothing else can—and opens us anew to the flow of grace."

No matter what happens in my life, whether I'm in recovery or I'm falling into the pit, whatever lies ahead for me, I know that I am saved by grace. He's giving me more courage every day to accept His acceptance. It's an acceptance not based on what I do or how I do it. It's acceptance not based on what I think of myself or what others think of me. It's an acceptance based on what He has done on the cross for me and how He accepts me as His own dearly loved child. As the Rev. Tony Campolo, former spiritual advisor to President Bill Clinton, used to say, "God's got a wallet with my picture in it!"

IN THE END

In the end, it all comes back to very simple principles. For me to have anything close to a happy and healthy life, I HAVE TO follow some specific rules about taking care of myself, starting with food intake. I keep trying to convince myself I am not a normal eater—that I can't eat what I want when I want to.

My adult life has been severely compromised by going way overboard with food. I have been on every diet known to man. I've tried pills from doctors, I've gone protein only, counted calories, food exchanges, and attended support groups. I've written "A" papers in graduate school on eating disorders and depression, trying to heal myself through knowledge. I've been to rehab four times, and had my stomach stapled twice.

I've spent hour upon hour in therapy trying to figure it all out. There is no doubt in my mind that the therapy helped. I gained some valuable awareness about myself and my family. But all the diets, support programs, and therapy still bring me back to square one.

During one of my periods of great weight loss, I was at a men's retreat sponsored by my wonderful church family. I met a gentleman who, after I shared my compelling story of weight loss and spiritual renewal, invited me to speak at his church. Never one to refuse an audience, I drove past the Pittsburgh International Airport to tiny Clinton, Pa. some weeks later to speak to a respectful crowd of about twenty adults.

The talk was scheduled in a board room, and I stood at one end of a long table, complete with my "before" and "after" photos, and a few notes as reference. I love such gatherings when I'm on my game. I ask God to speak through me so the people can perhaps hear something to enrich their life in some way. When God answers those prayers, I find that I, too, want to listen to what comes out of my mouth.

After a nice introduction, in a low-tone, I told this group that I had the secret to weight loss. I paused to create some suspense. God was going to have fun today, but He was also going to make sure I told the simple truth.

"The secret to weight loss is . . . to eat right and exercise," I confessed.

The small group appeared to let out a collective sigh, hoping for a simpler solution—maybe one of those infomercials that tell you to take a pill and eat as much as you want. HA!

Two-thirds of adults in our county are overweight and it's not because we don't know what to do—it's because we can't do what we know we have to do. The dieting industry makes billions trying to convince us that they alone have the way but the simple pyramid of food intake is right.

When someone steps up and loses weight, it's not because of the diet they're on as much as they have reached a point in their life when they are ready to do so. Every single time I've lost weight, I gave up the decision-making process to a sheet of paper with some form of healthy eating plan written down. The minute I start taking the decision-making power back, the minute I fancy in my mind that I am a normal eater, is precisely when relapse begins.

In a very real way, my "worship" of food keeps me from the God I should love. The more attention I give to spiritual matters, my life is inevitably better. Worship God, not food.

To do that requires a discipline that to this day I can't achieve on my own. I need the support of family, friends, doctors, and folks who share the same problem. At the very beginning of square one, I must start by asking for God's help. When I stray from these things, it's the beginning of trouble. When I look back on my life, my greatest achievement might be in the way I tried to help others who had struggles with weight and other issues in their lives.

Since I started writing this book in 2001, some of the concepts about food addiction have changed. The Diagnostic and Statistical Manual of Mental Disorders, Fifth Edition (DSM-5) has increased the number of eating disorders from five to eight, though there is no category specifically for food addiction. In psychological circles, there is thought that for some people, like me, the act of compulsive eating may be a behavioral addiction rather than linked with consumption of a specific food.

I exhibit such behavioral indicators, such as consuming greater quantities of food than I intended and eating certain foods (like sugars and bread) despite negative consequences. If it's a question of whether I'm addicted to food or addicted to the process of eating (loneliness, boredom), I'd say that I have an eating addiction.

Researchers can argue all they want about whether food is addicting or not. Part of the reason for writing this book is my argument that it can be. Arguments aside, call it addiction, compulsion, weak will, or anything you wish. You have read the destructive force that food has had in my life. When I ask for God's help, take things a day at a time, and follow my plan, things go fine. When I don't, well you can go back to Chapter "X" if you want.

You know the story.

I've learned so much on my journey. Exercise. A food plan. It all seems so simple. The biggest takeaway is that the hollowness of grief cannot be filled with pizza and potatoes. Yet that is my greatest struggle, no matter how much I follow food plans or embrace being in love with someone who truly loves me.

EPILOGUE

The Home Run – Zandy's Turn at Bat

The small house was totally dark as I pulled into the driveway late on Monday, August 8, 2016. I already knew. "Stay in the car," I told my daughter.

I ran to the porch, put the key in the lock, and burst through the door. As I switched on the overhead light, I began yelling. "Ed, Ed, Eddie, Eddie."

I wanted an answer, a groan, a something.

Before I could make the few steps from the front room to Ed's bedroom, his dog Charlie came out to greet me. I turned the corner into Ed's bedroom and hit the wall switch.

And there he was.

I ran back to the porch and shouted to my daughter.

I guess being a newspaper reporter has its advantages. I've always been able to remain calm during a crisis. I called 9-1-1, told them Ed's medical information, and that I couldn't get a pulse and thought he was dead.

I went back in to spend our last minutes alone. I gently scratched his back in the place where he often asked me to. I couldn't bear to try to see his face—I'd seen my mom a few hours after she'd died and I didn't want to remember him any way but with his beautiful blue eyes —the ones I'd called "striking" in the first newspaper story I wrote about him—looking out from behind his dark lashes.

With Penn Hills Volunteer Fire Department No. 7 just a block away, it didn't take long for help to arrive.

———

J ust a few months after our trip to South Carolina in 2016, Ed began to experience some periods of lightheadedness. In late May or early June, he visited Dr. Crossey to get checked out. The doctor switched a few medications and the change seemed to help.

As we sat watching TV the night after the visit, Ed handed me the office visit sheet that listed all his maladies. I guess time and sick family members had made me numb to the seriousness of these kind of lists, so I wouldn't have guessed that these illnesses would result in his death in just another two months. We decided I should write down the numerous diagnoses to drive home for this book what his body had been put through over the last several years.

He joked that his medical statistics were too numerous to fit on a baseball card: cellulitis, sepsis, sleep apnea and resulting heart valve damage, venous stasis, depression, morbid obesity, thrombophlebitis of deep veins of lower extremities, urinary incontinence, fatigue, vitamin B-12 deficiency, lymphedema, hypertension, atrial flutter, pulmonary hypertension, cardiomyopathy, hearing loss, wound, and MRSA.

That night, he wrote in our notes: "Surviving all this suffering and medical problems is a miracle in itself."

For his birthday on June 24, he posted on Facebook what, in retrospect, sounded like a farewell letter to his friends. He made a point of saying that he didn't plan on going anywhere anytime soon. But it added to my worries about him. Instead of going for a nice dinner to celebrate as we planned, he changed it a nearby restaurant and really didn't eat a lot. All week, he had wanted to go have a chocolate-dipped ice cream cone, but changed his mind about that, too. A few weeks later, after I jokingly told him I had been bummed we hadn't gone to get him the cone, he smiled and took us for one.

Ed became more persistent than ever that summer about us getting married. I was having some problems on my home front and I didn't want to make his problems worse by dragging him in to mine. And the more he mentioned it, the more I was frustrated by the never-ending request. Don't get me wrong. I wanted to spend our lives together. I was working hard to move some things forward so that we'd have the chance to get married. There are days now that I talk to him and say, "See, you should have just held on a bit more. It could have been ours."

Though we'd had disagreements, Ed and I only ever really had one fight and that was a few weeks before he died, when I was very late meeting him. I caught up with him at a local bar and it was obvious he'd already had quite a few drinks. He became argumentative about the marriage issue, pointing out that we didn't know how much time we had left to be together. I kept assuring him that it would happen but that we needed to work out the logistics. He raised his voice at me, enough that when I saw the bartender, Gloria, a few days later at the local supermarket, she mentioned it.

Ed told me later that week that he'd quit being angry about the marriage issue and actually gave me a greeting card that said how much he loved me, even if we weren't at the same place.

I noticed that we'd been staying in instead of going out, except for our Saturday night dinners. More than once, he got dizzy while walking and had to pause, or even sit a few minutes, before proceeding to the car. Much as I got tired of the wedding issue, he probably got tired of hearing me say, "Go to the doctor."

On Wednesday, August 3, 2016, Ed called me at work and said, "Hey, Web MD, what causes a rumbling rectum?" We both kind of laughed and I told him I'd check it out. I went online and found a few causes.

"Well, it could be gas, an infection . . . or worse, a rupture or cancer," I told him. I asked him a few more questions and then suggested that he contact Dr. Crossey.

I went over to his house Thursday evening. I asked how he was feeling and he said, aside from some diarrhea, he was okay. We made plans for Saturday. I encouraged him to see the doctor.

When Saturday came, there was another family issue, so again I was late for our date. Ed seemed more sad than angry. We always had dinner together on Saturdays. Ed just started driving, as we often did, meandering past some of the places we ate frequently. It was an odd route, and we ended up at a spaghetti restaurant he liked.

As we headed toward the car after our meal, he really struggled with the lightheadedness. When we reached the parking lot, he literally draped himself across the car hood. It took him several minutes to recover. I asked if he wanted me to drive, but he said no.

When we got to his place, I crawled to the wall side of his bed so we could lie down and watch TV together. He stopped to go to the bathroom and when he came in, instead of plopping down on his side, he sat on the edge and leaned his head back onto my waist as I laid sideways, forming a T. He seemed peaceful as I stroked his hair for what seemed like an hour. He asked a few times if I was ok, knowing that his weight might hurt. I reassured him, and enjoyed this moment of togetherness that broke the pattern of what we usually did.

It would be our last date night.

On Sunday evening, I had to run an errand. On the way back, I called Ed and asked if he wanted me to bring him something from out.

"Coffee," he said. Always black.

When I showed up, he looked tired—in retrospect, almost in an angelic way. I figured it was because he had been at the softball league playoffs that day but I learned later that he never went out. He sat up in bed and I sat beside him. We talked, but not about anything memorable. It was already 10:30 and I told him I had to go home to get ready for bed.

Ed pulled me in for a hug, but it was unlike any we'd ever had. He held me close, cheek to cheek, me standing, him sitting, for more than five minutes. It was like he didn't want to let me go. And when it ended, he pulled me in for a gentle kiss. Our last moments together—how this has helped me to deal with the grief and missing him. In retrospect, I think he knew.

The next afternoon, I called him at 4:30 as I left work. We talked at this time nearly every day. I got no answer. Knowing that he sometimes napped after work, I didn't give it much thought. I had an errand to run that evening with my daughter and when repeated attempts to reach him by phone, text, and Facebook failed, I grew very worried. We stopped at his house on the way back home.

———

I put Charlie in the now-vacant bedroom that had been used by Ed's mom. The firefighters were the first to arrive, and they confirmed that he was gone. I learned later that he'd called off work, telling his supervisor that he'd be in later if he felt better.

The police arrived and then the paramedics. I asked about calling his family and they said they'd let me know when to do that. I wanted to call his brother, Lee, but I waited as instructed and tried to absorb the finality of it all.

Fortunately, Ed's friend Kyle Jenkins and his wife, Janet, arrived after getting a call from a member of the softball league who'd heard the 9-1-1 dispatch come in over the emergency radio. They were worried that Ed's mother was there alone. They didn't know she had moved out almost a year before. Thankfully, they stayed until the end that evening, comforting Ed's family, me, and my son, who had arrived once my daughter called him. My daughter was exhausted from taking care of her father and had fallen asleep in the car, so I let her sleep through all the commotion.

I talked to the medical examiner and related Ed's medical history. Then I called Lee. It was probably the hardest call I've ever made in my life. I have no memory of what I said but I do remember Lee's shock at the news. Soon after, Pat O'Connor, the husband of Ed's sister, Jody, arrived. He was a lineman for the electric company and happened to be in the area. He rushed past everyone with a look of disbelief on his face. (Sadly, Pat died just seven months later.) Soon after, the rest of Ed's family arrived.

I hung outside with Janet and my son, wanting to give the family some privacy. The funeral director came and I was so thankful that they treated Ed's body with respect as they escorted him to the waiting car.

In their own grief, Ed's family generously included me in the funeral planning. I wondered if I'd be listed in the obituary and was heartened that I was listed as "loving companion." I regretted that I would never be remembered as his fiancée or his wife.

People from softball, church, high school, the college, and the community poured into the funeral home on the main road through Penn Hills, just a stone's throw from his home. When Dr. Crossey arrived to pay his final respects, I asked him what he thought was the cause of death. Without hesitation, he said, "Heart attack."

Ed's funeral service was held at Hebron Church. I purposely sat on his favorite side, about seven rows back, like he always did. Doug Rehberg conducted the service. The eulogies from those close to him through the years painted a picture of his "heart of gold" as they shared their remembrances from childhood, church, family, and sports. Kyle's remarks included the Facebook post Ed had shared on his birthday, the farewell address he delivered just a little more than six weeks before he died to his more than 1,200 Facebook friends. It said, in part:

> *. . . The larger reason for my waxing philosophic today is that, without a single doubt, one of the best things in my life is the Olympic-quality support system I have—and that would be YOUR FAULT. The family and friends around me are nothing short of incredible. No matter what's going on in my life, I could always turn to a slew of you folks—anytime, anywhere.*
>
> *As I re-read what I have written, it sounds like a resignation letter or a goodbye message. Well, I ain't goin' nowhere until the Good Lord calls. I guess I've fallen prey to the birthday milestone, take stock of your life thing. It just all needed to be said today.*

In short, I love and appreciate all of you for what you bring to my life . . . know it, understand it and for goodness sakes don't stop. If you're reading this, I'm afraid you're in.

God bless and feeling every bit of 57 today.

Ed

As great as he was at sports in his youth, it's obvious to me now that Ed was not put on this Earth to play baseball. He would have never touched the lives of his stadium fans the way he did the fans of Ed, the caring, loving, giving, sweet, tender, sensitive, compassionate, thoughtful son, brother, uncle, nephew, friend, teacher, mentor, and counselor.

He was put on Earth to be the listening ear, the advisor, the comforter, the guy who handed you $100 when you were down, the man who literally saved a few lives, the one who lifted your spirit with a joke or kind words, the one who looked at you with those beautiful blue eyes that let you know every word out of his mouth, except when it came to his food addiction, was sincere and from his heart.

What he didn't understand—and what those who knew him took for granted as just being Ed without understanding why—is that God may have derailed his baseball dreams and instead given him a big body. Ed needed it. Where else could he house and nourish his large and giving heart that touched so many lives?

As a journalist for more than four decades, I've become somewhat of a skeptic. But I've always had an open mind about signs from those who have passed away. In the weeks and months after Ed's death, he seemed to be reaching out: butterflies, dragonflies, rainbows, seeing his numbers "23" and "32," and having my phone jump to his family's phone numbers while I was on another call (which still happens).

There was even a dog that approached me in the cemetery when I was visiting Ed's grave on the first Christmas he was gone. The dog's owner was nowhere in sight. As I talked to the dog and petted him, the owner suddenly appeared. I asked him the dog's name and I was shocked when he said, "Charlie." Just like Ed's dog.

"Charlie" reappeared with his owner on Thanksgiving Day 2017 and again on April 20, 2018, the day Ed and I considered our anniversary because it was the day he confessed he had feelings for me. I only saw "Charlie" on those special days, never any other time during my nearly weekly visits to Ed's grave.

On the second anniversary of Ed's death, as his family, Doug Rehberg, and I gathered to share stories at his grave, I told a few people about "Charlie" helping to make those days a little easier because he appeared to be a sign. As if on cue, as Doug was telling us about Jesus accepting us as we are, "Charlie" wandered over to our group until his owner called him away.

But the most indisputable sign from beyond came in the strangest of places about two months after Ed died. I was eating lunch in the dining hall of the Sisters of Mercy Convent in the Oakland section of Pittsburgh, across the driveway from my office.

As my four co-workers and I were talking, I heard and felt a powerful "whoosh," a rush of air close to my left ear. "Ed," I said to myself. I just knew that it was him. No one else heard it or reacted. And I didn't share because I really didn't know how to explain what had just happened.

There was something strangely familiar about that sound. Yet I couldn't put my finger on it. I had looked around when it happened. There were no people walking by. No open windows. No air conditioning. No heating vents nearby. It wasn't like what happens when my ears pop going down a mountain or taking off in a plane.

For nearly two months, I tried to identify the sound. And then, I guess you could say it hit me. It was the sound of a baseball as it cuts through the air.

I had always wanted to see Ed hit a ball but never had that chance. What better way to let me know that his body was now free of the weight and pain that kept him from his passion for most of the last four decades.

I closed my eyes and pictured Ed as he was in high school, in perfect form, in his red-and-gold trimmed Penn Hills uniform, standing at home plate with his dad on the pitcher's mound. Keeping his eyes on the ball, his back foot planted, striding right at the pitcher, and executing a level swing with a wooden bat, just as Ace had taught him.

In my imagination, I heard Ed's dad say: "Let her hear what you've got, boy."

Cr-rack . . . Whoosh.

NEED HELP?

If you are struggling with an eating or food addiction, or behavioral health issues, information is available at the websites below or by contacting a local mental health provider:

Substance Abuse and Mental Health Services Administration (SAMHSA)
https://www.samhsa.gov/

National Alliance on Mental Illness (NAMI)
https://www.nami.org

Mental Health America
www.mentalhealthamerica.net

ABOUT THE AUTHORS

(Photo by FineLine Weddings, courtesy Heidi and Jonathan Winkler)

Ed Adams, MSW, earned a master of social work degree from the University of Pittsburgh. He worked as a sociology/psychology instructor and student support specialist at Community College of Allegheny County in Monroeville, Pa.

Zandy Dudiak is an award-winning journalist, who currently works in nonprofit communications and as a freelance writer in Pittsburgh, Pa.

For more information visit
https://www.facebook.com/EdAdamsDyingtoEat/

Made in the USA
Columbia, SC
23 January 2019